CLARENCE LARKIN

CHARTS COLLECTION

CLARENCE LARKIN

GRAPEVINE BOOKS

Published by

GRAPEVINE BOOKS

www.grapevinebooks.com

email: contact@grapevinebooks.com

Ordering Information:

Quantity sales: Special discounts are available on quantity purchases by corporations, associations, and others.

For details, reach out to the publisher.

First published by Grapevine Books, 2026

CONTENTS

Clarence Larkin Charts Collection

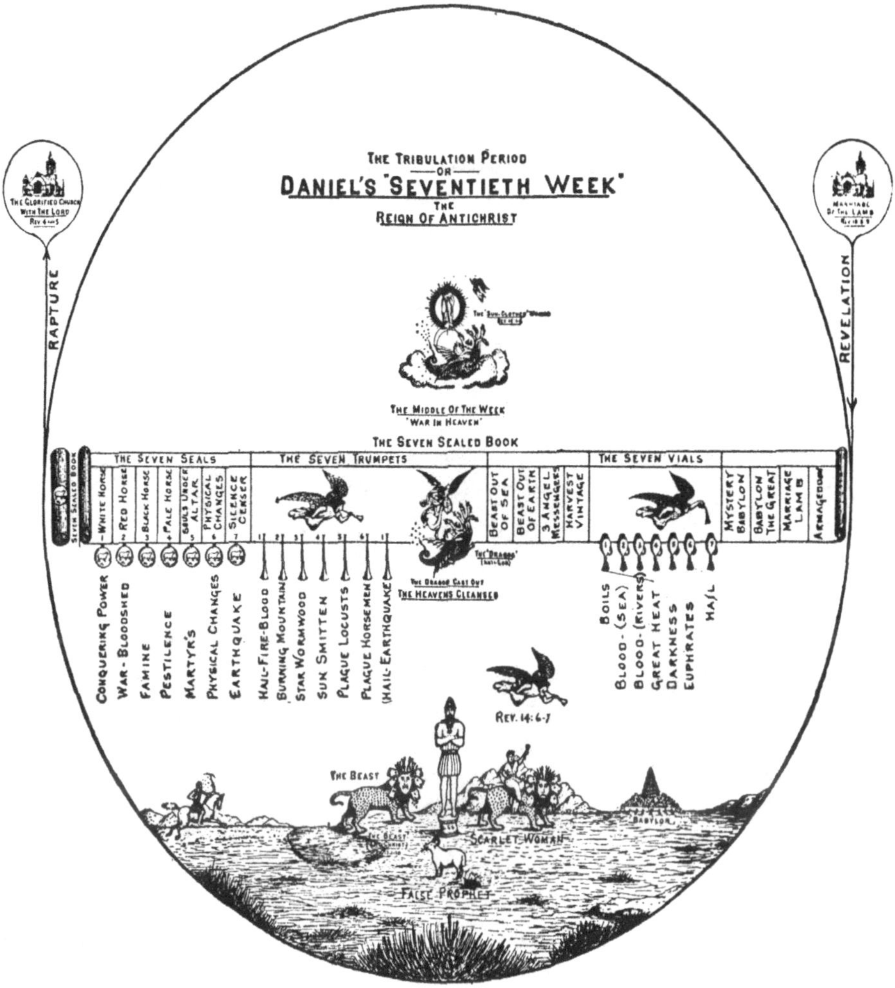

THE TRIBULATION
(JUDGMENT)

THE SIX DAYS O
FIRST DAY
COSMIC LIGHT
SECOND DAY
FIRMAMENT FORMED
THIRD DAY
TWO WORKS
THE LAND REAPPEARS | VEGETATION REAPPEARS
GEN. 1:3-5
3 And God said, Let there be light: and there was light.
4 And God saw the light, that it was good: and God divided the light from the darkness.
5 And God called the light Day, and the darkness he called Night. And the evening and the morning were the first day.
GEN. 1:6-8
6 ¶ And God said, Let there be a firmament in the midst of the waters, and let it divide the waters from the waters.
7 And God made the firmament, and divided the waters which were under the firmament from the waters which were above the firmament: and it was so.
8 And God called the firmament Heaven. And the evening and the morning were the second day.
GEN. 1:9-10
FIRST WORK
9 ¶ And God said, Let the waters under the heaven be gathered together unto one place, and let the dry land appear: and it was so.
10 And God called the dry land Earth; and the gathering together of the waters called he Seas: and God saw that it was good.
GEN. 1:11-13
SECOND WORK
11 And God said, Let the earth bring forth grass, the herb yielding seed, and the fruit tree yielding fruit after his kind, whose seed is in itself, upon the earth: and it was so.
12 And the earth brought forth grass, and herb yielding seed after his kind, and the tree yielding fruit, whose seed was in itself, after his kind: and God saw that it was good.
13 And the evening and the morning were the third day.
DESIGNED AND DRAWN
BY CLARENCE LARKIN
FOXCHASE, PHIL'A., PA
COPYRIGHTED
1|20|1920

RE-CREATION

FOURTH DAY
SOLAR LIGHT RESTORED

GEN. 1:14-19

14 ¶ And God said, Let there be lights in the firmament of the heaven to divide the day from the night; and let them be for signs, and for seasons, and for days, and years:

15 And let them be for lights in the firmament of the heaven to give light upon the earth: and it was so.

16 And God made two great lights; the greater light to rule the day, and the lesser light to rule the night: *he made* the stars also.

17 And God set them in the firmament of the heaven to give light upon the earth,

18 And to rule over the day and over the night, and to divide the light from the darkness: and God saw that *it was* good.

19 And the evening and the morning were the fourth day.

FIFTH DAY
CREATION OF FISH AND FOWL

GEN. 1:20-23

20 And God said, Let the waters bring forth abundantly the moving creature that hath life, and fowl *that* may fly above the earth in the open firmament of heaven.

21 And God created great whales, and every living creature that moveth, which the waters brought forth abundantly, after their kind, and every winged fowl after his kind: and God saw that *it was* good.

22 And God blessed them, saying, Be fruitful, and multiply, and fill the waters in the seas, and let fowl multiply in the earth.

23 And the evening and the morning were the fifth day.

SIXTH DAY
TWO WORKS
CREATION OF ANIMALS | CREATION OF MAN

GEN. 1:24-25
FIRST WORK

24 ¶ And God said, Let the earth bring forth the living creature after his kind, cattle, and creeping thing, and beast of the earth after his kind: and it was so.

25 And God made the beast of the earth after his kind, and cattle after their kind, and every thing that creepeth upon the earth after his kind: and God saw that *it was* good.

GEN. 1:26-31
SECOND WORK

26 ¶ And God said, Let us make man in our image, after our likeness: and let them have dominion over the fish of the sea, and over the fowl of the air, and over the cattle, and over all the earth, and over every creeping thing that creepeth upon the earth.

27 So God created man in his *own* image, in the image of God created he him; male and female created he them.

28 And God blessed them, and God said unto them, Be fruitful, and multiply, and replenish the earth, and subdue it: and have dominion over the fish of the sea, and over the fowl of the air, and over every living thing that moveth upon the earth.

31 And God saw every thing that he had made, and, behold, *it was* very good. And the evening and the morning were the sixth day.

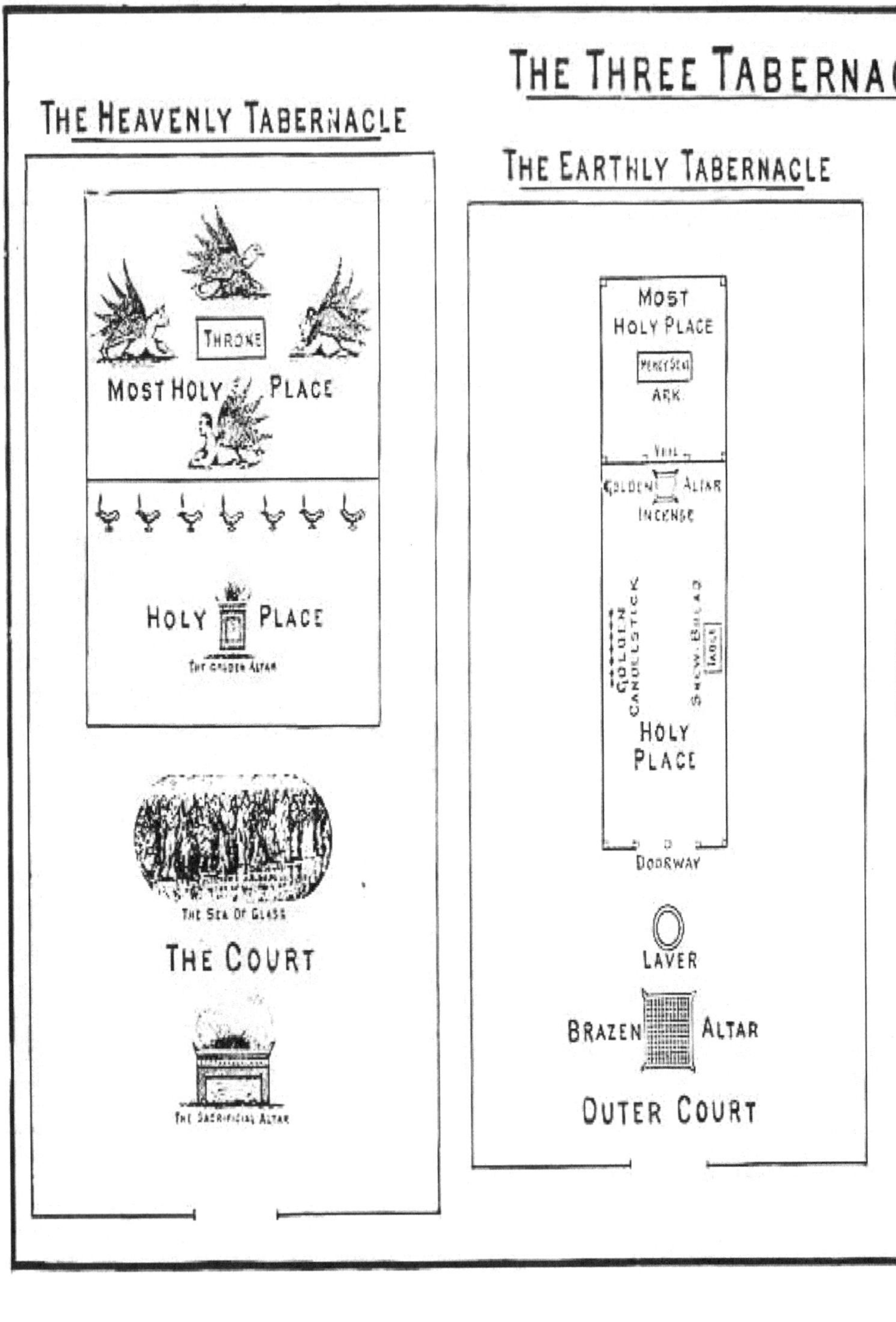
THE THREE TABERNA
THE HEAVENLY TABERNACLE
THRONE
MOST HOLY PLACE
HOLY PLACE
THE GOLDEN ALTAR
THE SEA OF GLASS
THE COURT
THE SACRIFICIAL ALTAR
THE EARTHLY TABERNACLE
MOST HOLY PLACE
MERCY SEAT
ARK
VEIL
GOLDEN ALTAR
INCENSE
GOLDEN CANDLESTICK
SHEW-BREAD
TABLE
HOLY PLACE
DOORWAY
LAVER
BRAZEN ALTAR
OUTER COURT

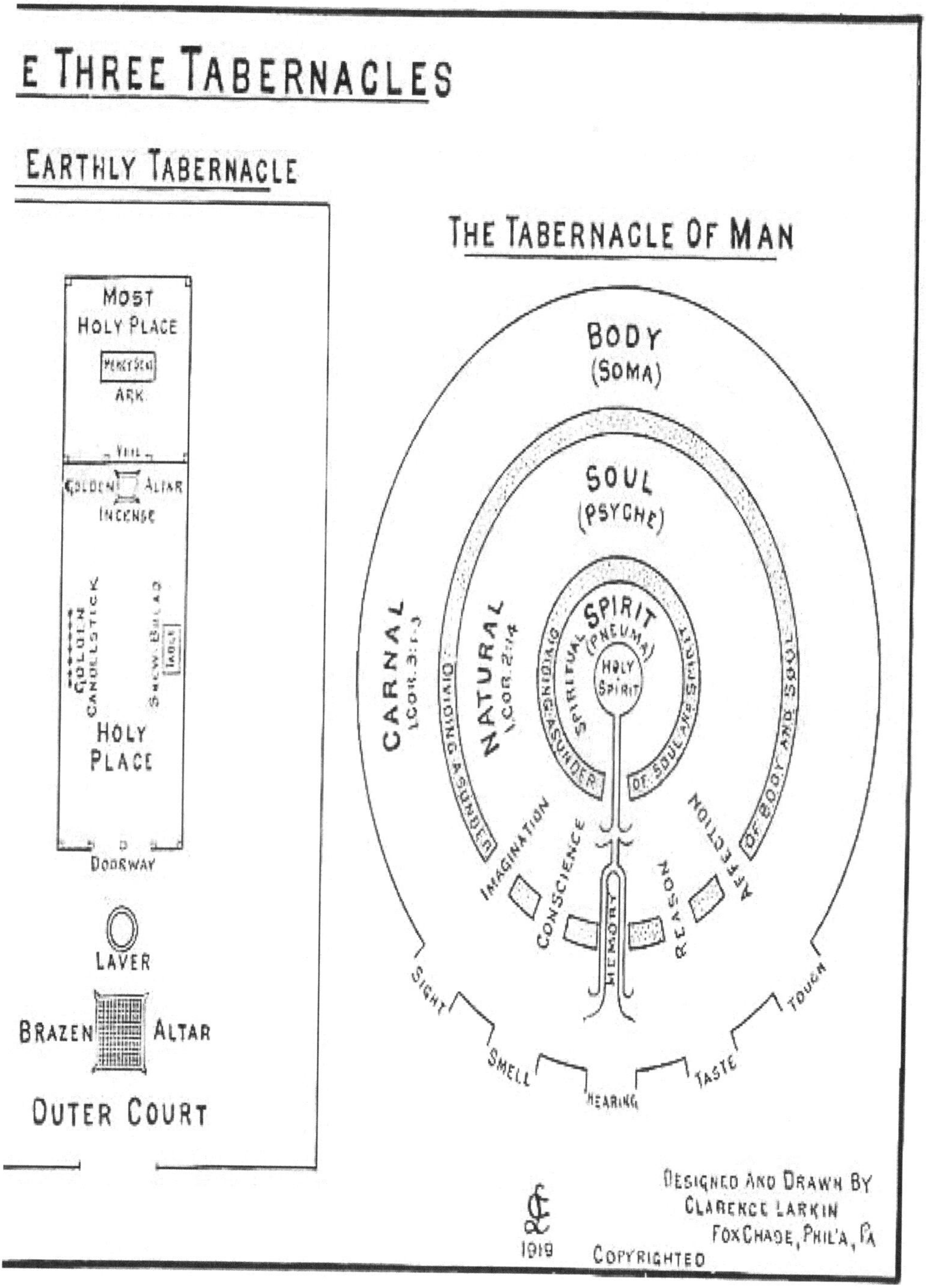
E THREE TABERNACLES
EARTHLY TABERNACLE
MOST
HOLY PLACE
ARK
VEIL
GOLDEN ALTAR
INCENSE
GOLDEN CANDLESTICK
SHEW-BREAD
TABLE
HOLY
PLACE
DOORWAY
LAVER
BRAZEN ALTAR
OUTER COURT
THE TABERNACLE OF MAN
BODY
(SOMA)
SOUL
(PSYCHE)
SPIRIT
(PNEUMA)
HOLY
SPIRIT
CARNAL
1 COR. 3:1-3
NATURAL
1 COR. 2:14
SPIRITUAL
DIVIDING ASUNDER
DIVIDING ASUNDER OF SOUL AND SPIRIT
OF BODY AND SOUL
IMAGINATION
CONSCIENCE
MEMORY
REASON
AFFECTION
SIGHT
SMELL
HEARING
TASTE
TOUCH
DESIGNED AND DRAWN BY
CLARENCE LARKIN
FOX CHASE, PHIL'A, PA
1919
COPYRIGHTED

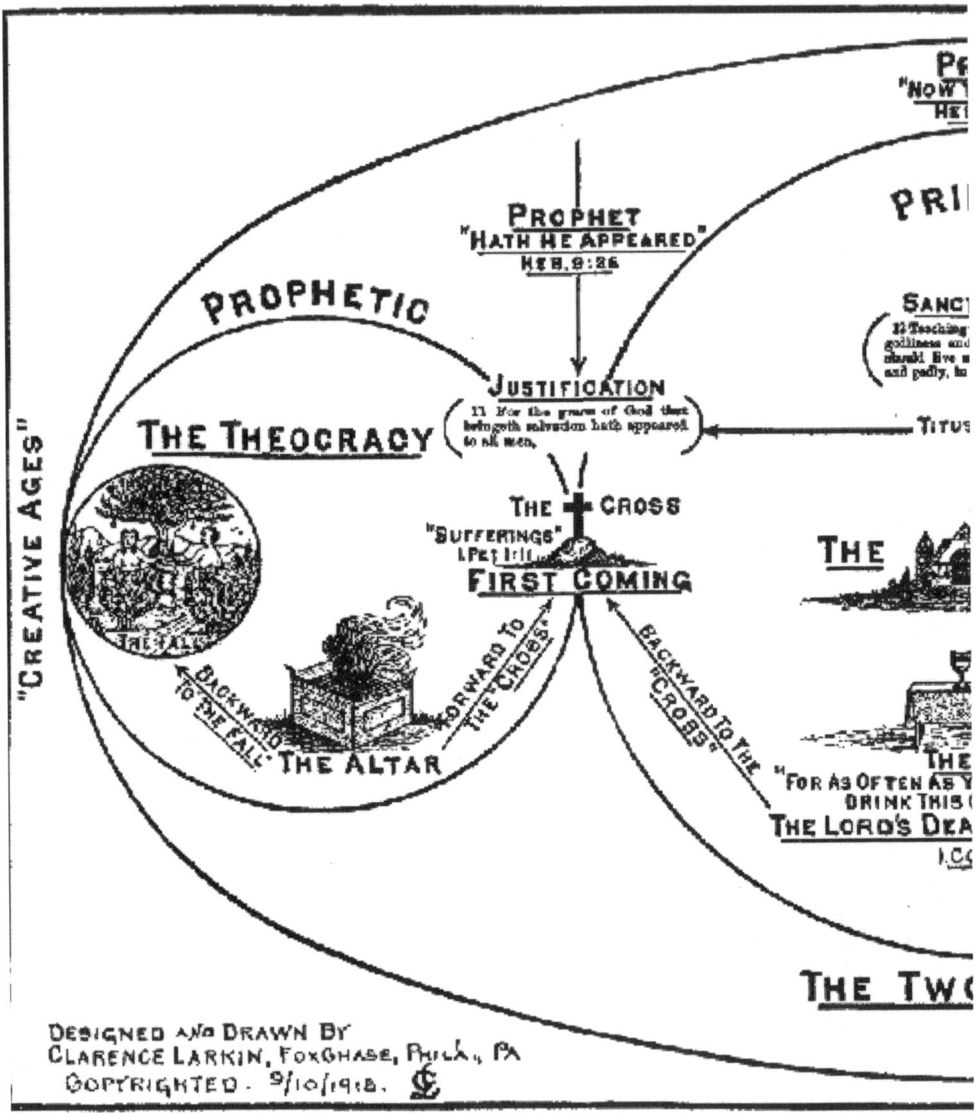
"CREATIVE AGES"
PROPHETIC
PROPHET
"HATH HE APPEARED"
HEB. 9:26
JUSTIFICATION
11 For the grace of God that bringeth salvation hath appeared to all men,
THE THEOCRACY
THE FALL
THE CROSS
"SUFFERINGS"
I. PET. 1:11
FIRST COMING
BACKWARD TO THE FALL
FORWARD TO THE "CROSS"
THE ALTAR
BACKWARD TO THE "CROSS"
TITUS
"FOR AS OFTEN AS Y
DRINK THIS
THE LORD'S DEA
THE TW
DESIGNED AND DRAWN BY
CLARENCE LARKIN, FOXCHASE, PHILA., PA
COPYRIGHTED. 9/10/1918.

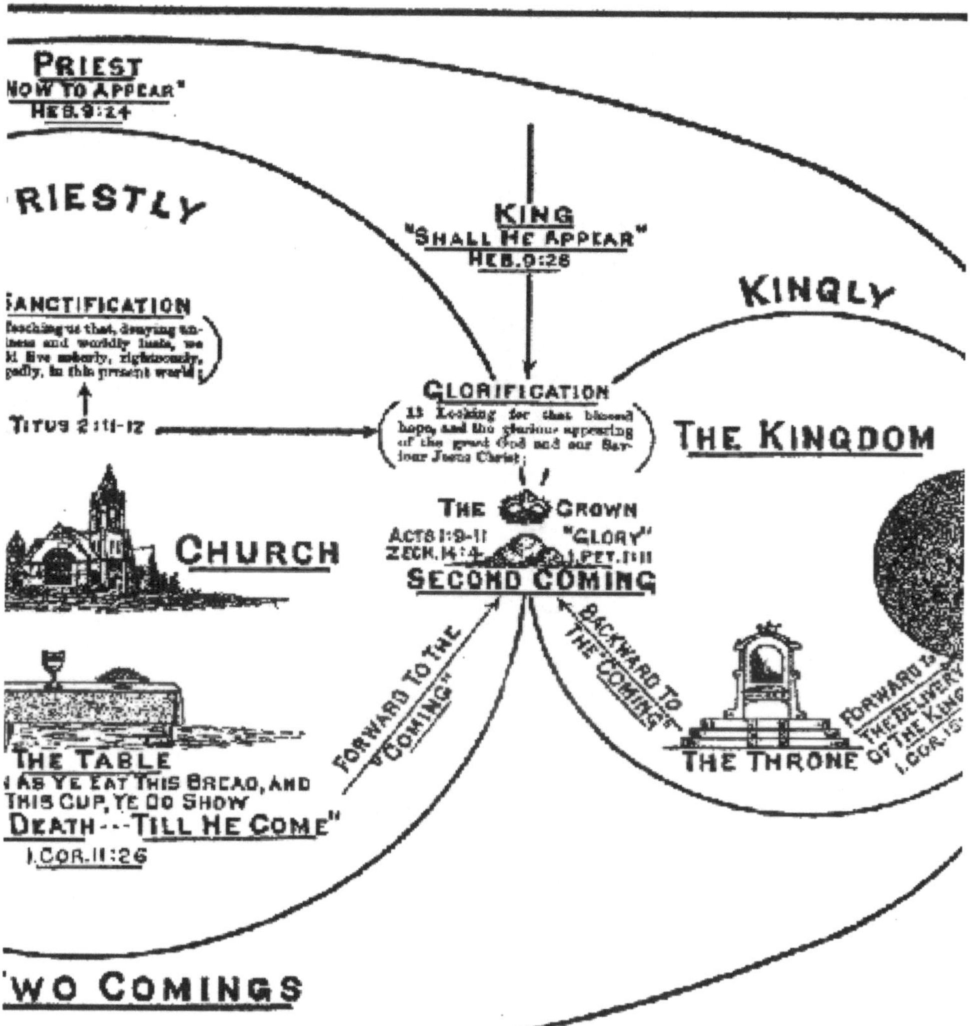
PRIEST
"NOW TO APPEAR"
HEB. 9:24
RIESTLY
KING
"SHALL HE APPEAR"
HEB. 9:28
KINGLY
SANCTIFICATION
TITUS 2:11-12
GLORIFICATION
13 Looking for that blessed hope, and the glorious appearing of the great God and our Saviour Jesus Christ;
THE KINGDOM
THE CROWN
ACTS 1:9-11
ZECH. 14:4
"GLORY"
I. PET. 1:11
CHURCH
SECOND COMING
FORWARD TO THE "COMING"
BACKWARD TO THE "COMING"
THE TABLE
AS YE EAT THIS BREAD, AND THIS CUP, YE DO SHOW DEATH---TILL HE COME"
I. COR. 11:26
THE THRONE
WO COMINGS

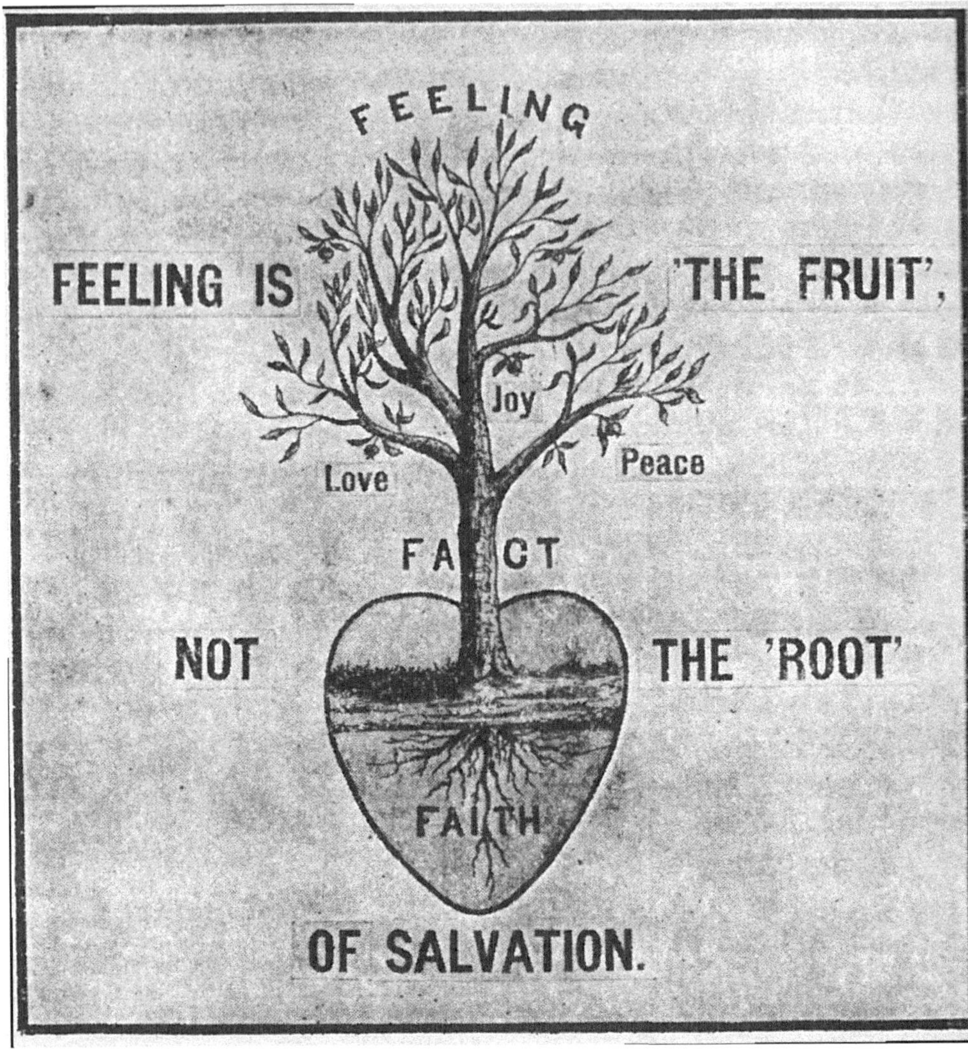
FEELING
FEELING IS
'THE FRUIT',
Joy
Love
Peace
FACT
NOT
THE 'ROOT'
FAITH
OF SALVATION.

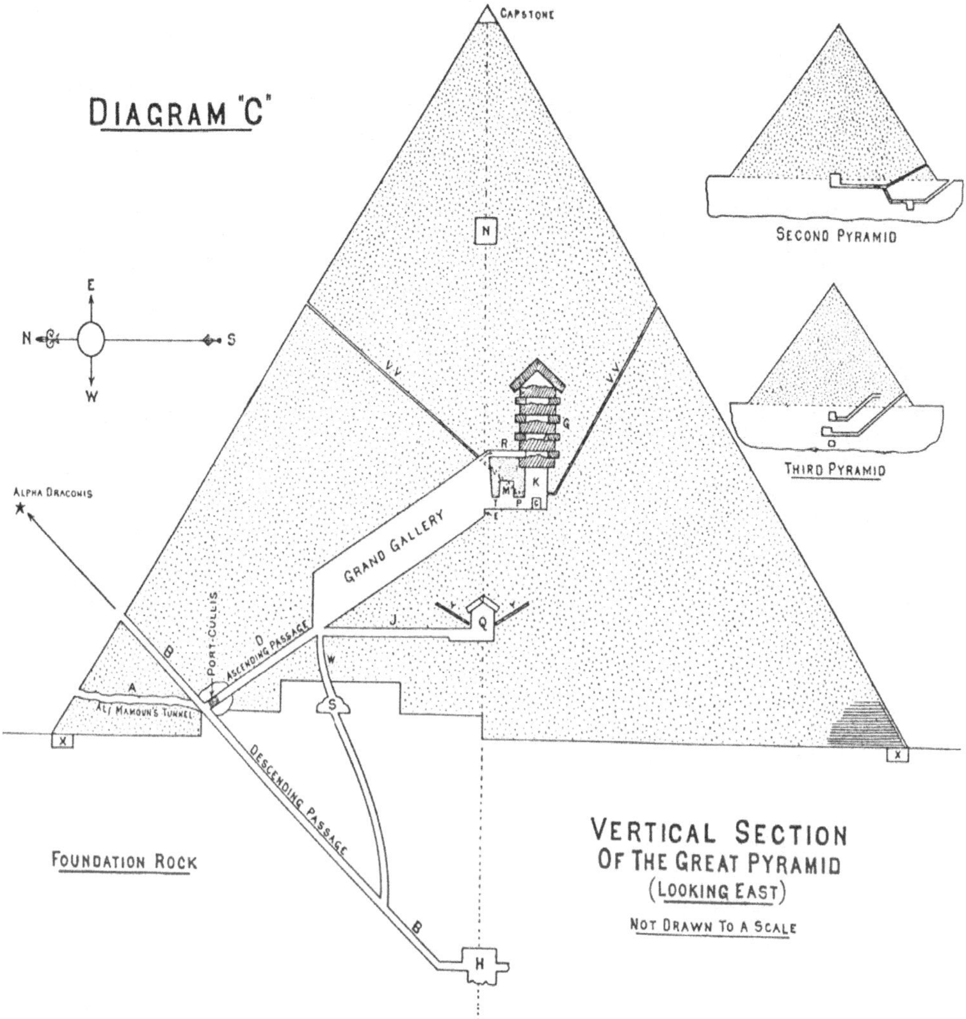
CAPSTONE
DIAGRAM "C"
N
E
N
S
W
V V
V V
G
R
K
M
T
P
C
E
ALPHA DRACONIS
GRAND GALLERY
ASCENDING PASSAGE
PORT-CULLIS
D
J
Q
W
B
A
ALI MAMOUN'S TUNNEL
S
X
X
DESCENDING PASSAGE
B
H
FOUNDATION ROCK
VERTICAL SECTION
OF THE GREAT PYRAMID
(LOOKING EAST)
NOT DRAWN TO A SCALE
SECOND PYRAMID
THIRD PYRAMID

When The New Testament Books Were Written

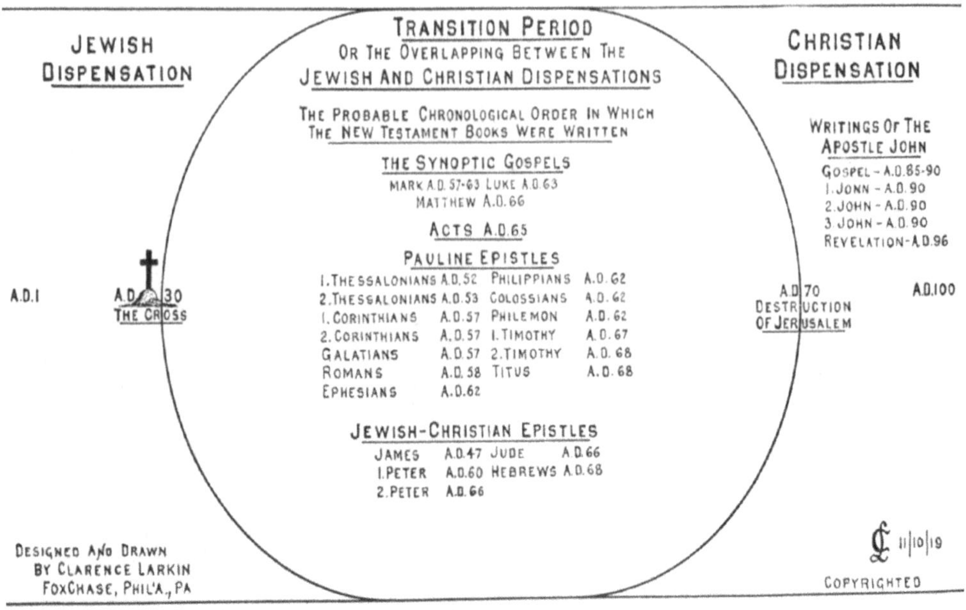

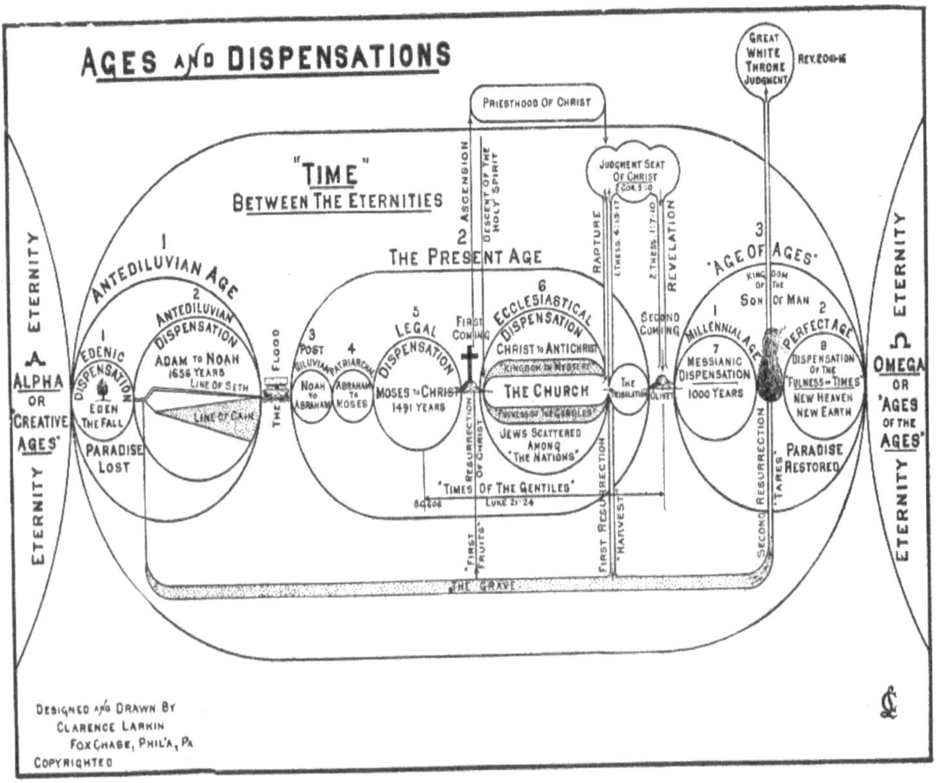

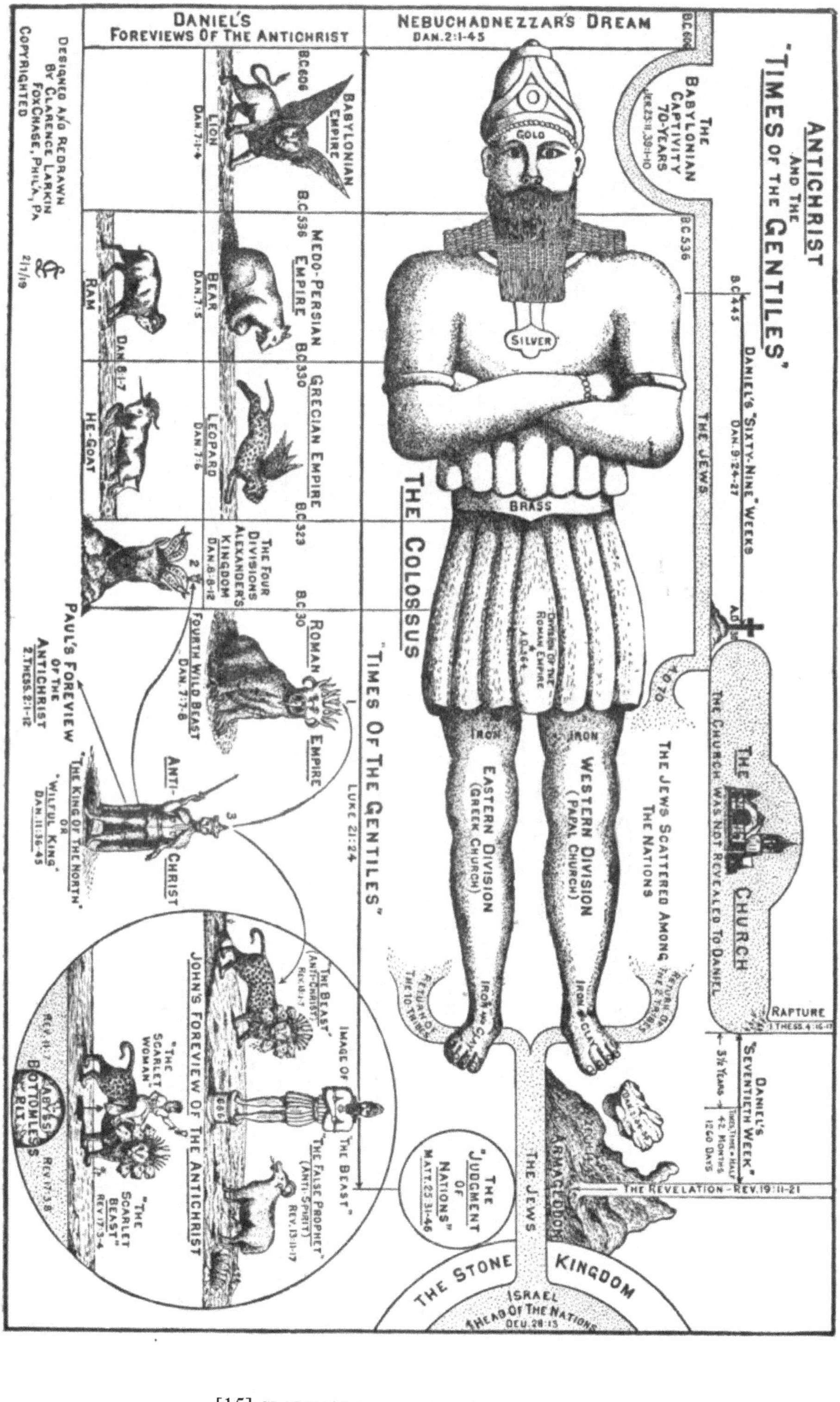
ANTICHRIST AND THE "TIMES OF THE GENTILES"
NEBUCHADNEZZAR'S DREAM
DAN. 2:1-45
DANIEL'S FOREVIEWS OF THE ANTICHRIST
B.C. 606
THE BABYLONIAN CAPTIVITY 70-YEARS
B.C. 536
B.C. 445
DANIEL'S "SIXTY-NINE" WEEKS
DAN. 9:24-27
THE JEWS
GOLD
SILVER
BRASS
IRON
IRON & CLAY
THE COLOSSUS
DIVISION OF THE ROMAN EMPIRE A.D. 364
WESTERN DIVISION (PAPAL CHURCH)
EASTERN DIVISION (GREEK CHURCH)
A.D. 70
THE JEWS SCATTERED AMONG THE NATIONS
THE CHURCH
THE CHURCH WAS NOT REVEALED TO DANIEL
RAPTURE
1 THESS. 4:16-17
DANIEL'S "SEVENTIETH WEEK"
3½ YEARS
42 MONTHS
1260 DAYS
THE REVELATION - REV. 19:11-21
ARMAGEDDON
THE "JUDGMENT OF NATIONS"
MATT. 25:31-46
THE JEWS
THE STONE KINGDOM
ISRAEL HEAD OF THE NATIONS
DEU. 28:13
"TIMES OF THE GENTILES"
LUKE 21:24
BABYLONIAN EMPIRE
LION
DAN. 7:1-4
MEDO-PERSIAN EMPIRE
BEAR
DAN. 7:5
RAM
DAN. 8:1-7
GRECIAN EMPIRE
B.C. 330
LEOPARD
DAN. 7:6
HE-GOAT
B.C. 323
THE FOUR DIVISIONS ALEXANDER'S KINGDOM
DAN. 8:8-12
ROMAN EMPIRE
B.C. 30
FOURTH WILD BEAST
DAN. 7:7-8
ANTI-CHRIST
"THE KING OF THE NORTH" OR "WILFUL KING"
DAN. 11:36-45
PAUL'S FOREVIEW OF THE ANTICHRIST
2 THESS. 2:1-12
JOHN'S FOREVIEW OF THE ANTICHRIST
"THE BEAST" (ANTI-CHRIST)
REV. 13:1-7
IMAGE OF THE BEAST
"THE FALSE PROPHET" (ANTI-SPIRIT)
REV. 13:11-17
"THE SCARLET WOMAN"
"THE SCARLET BEAST"
REV. 17:3-4
ABYSS BOTTOMLESS PIT
REV. 17:8
DESIGNED AND REDRAWN BY CLARENCE LARKIN FOX CHASE, PHILA., PA.
COPYRIGHTED
2/1/19

DIAGRAM OF THE EIGHT WORKS OF THE SIX DAYS

LIGHT	FIRMAMENT	LAND	VEGETATION	SUN	FISH	BEASTS	MAN
FIRMAMENT	LAND	VEGETATION	SUN	FISH	BEASTS	MAN	LIGHT
LAND	VEGETATION	SUN	FISH	BEASTS	MAN	LIGHT	FIRMAMENT
VEGETATION	SUN	FISH	BEASTS	MAN	LIGHT	FIRMAMENT	LAND
SUN	FISH	BEASTS	MAN	LIGHT	FIRMAMENT	LAND	VEGETATION
FISH	BEASTS	MAN	LIGHT	FIRMAMENT	LAND	VEGETATION	SUN
BEASTS	MAN	LIGHT	FIRMAMENT	LAND	VEGETATION	SUN	FISH
MAN	LIGHT	FIRMAMENT	LAND	VEGETATION	SUN	FISH	BEASTS

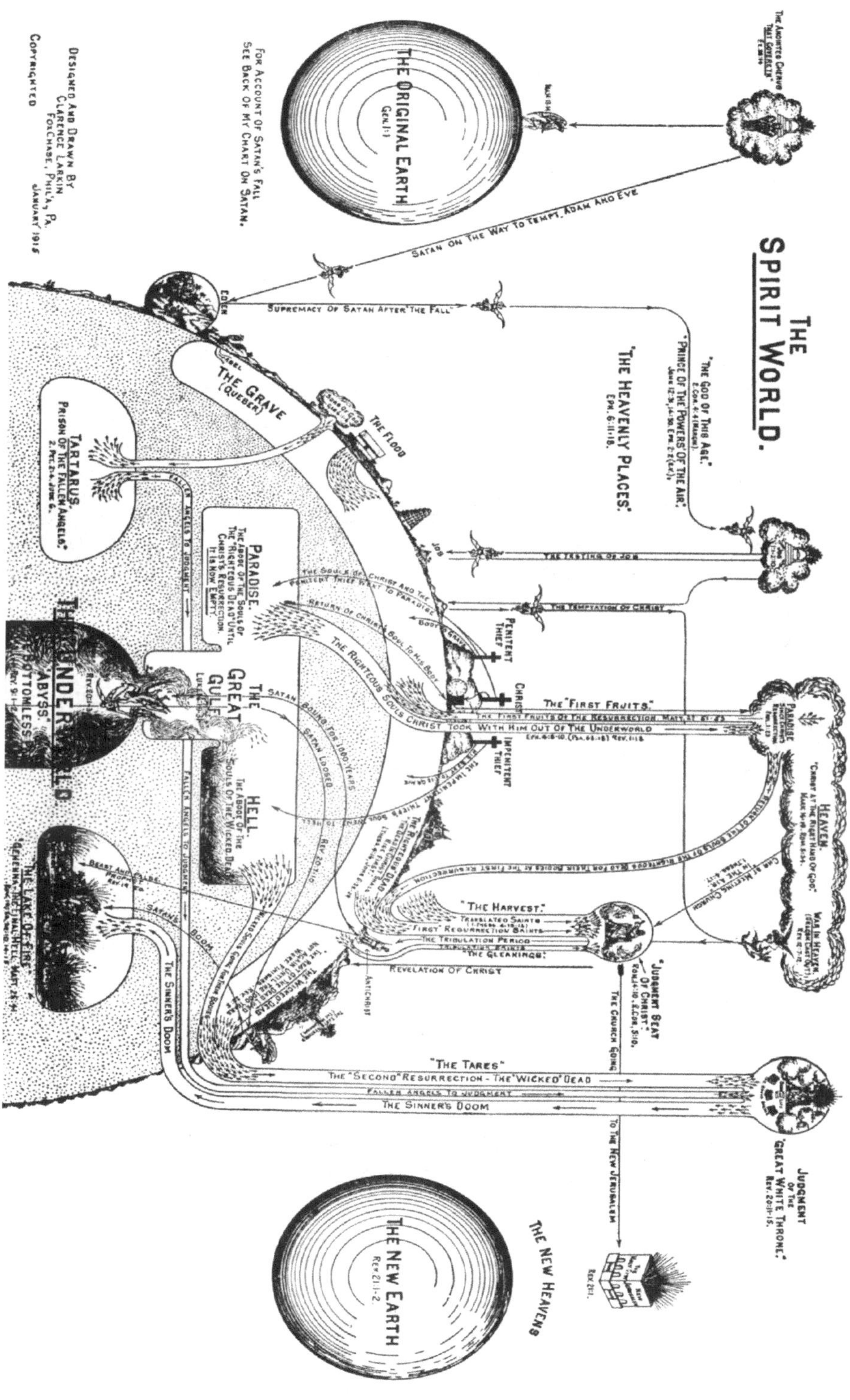
THE SPIRIT WORLD.
"THE GOD OF THIS AGE."
"PRINCE OF THE POWERS OF THE AIR."
"THE HEAVENLY PLACES."
EPH. 6:11-18.
THE ORIGINAL EARTH
GEN. 1:1
FOR ACCOUNT OF SATAN'S FALL SEE BACK OF MY CHART ON SATAN.
DESIGNED AND DRAWN BY CLARENCE LARKIN FOX CHASE, PHILA., PA.
COPYRIGHTED JANUARY 1918
SATAN ON THE WAY TO TEMPT ADAM AND EVE
SUPREMACY OF SATAN AFTER THE FALL
EDEN
THE GRAVE
(QUEBER)
THE FLOOD
TARTARUS
PRISON OF THE FALLEN ANGELS.
PARADISE
THE ABODE OF THE SOULS OF THE "RIGHTEOUS DEAD" UNTIL CHRIST'S RESURRECTION. IT IS NOW EMPTY.
THE TESTING OF JOB
JOB
THE TEMPTATION OF CHRIST
PENITENT THIEF
CHRIST
IMPENITENT THIEF
THE "FIRST FRUITS."
THE FIRST FRUITS OF THE RESURRECTION. MATT. 27:51-53
THE RIGHTEOUS SOULS CHRIST TOOK WITH HIM OUT OF THE UNDERWORLD
THE GREAT GULF
THE UNDERWORLD
"ABYSS."
BOTTOMLESS
HELL
THE ABODE OF THE SOULS OF THE WICKED DEAD.
SATAN BOUND FOR 1000 YEARS
SATAN LOOSED
FALLEN ANGELS TO JUDGMENT
HEAVEN
"CHRIST AT THE RIGHT HAND OF GOD."
WAR IN HEAVEN.
"THE HARVEST."
TRANSLATED SAINTS
"FIRST" RESURRECTION SAINTS
THE TRIBULATION PERIOD
"THE GLEANINGS."
REVELATION OF CHRIST
ANTICHRIST
"JUDGMENT SEAT OF CHRIST."
THE CHURCH GOING TO THE NEW JERUSALEM
"THE LAKE OF FIRE"
SATAN'S DOOM
THE SINNER'S DOOM
"THE TARES"
THE "SECOND" RESURRECTION - THE "WICKED" DEAD
FALLEN ANGELS TO JUDGMENT
THE SINNER'S DOOM
JUDGMENT OF THE "GREAT WHITE THRONE."
REV. 20:11-15.
THE NEW HEAVENS
THE NEW EARTH
REV. 21:1-2.
REV. 21:1.

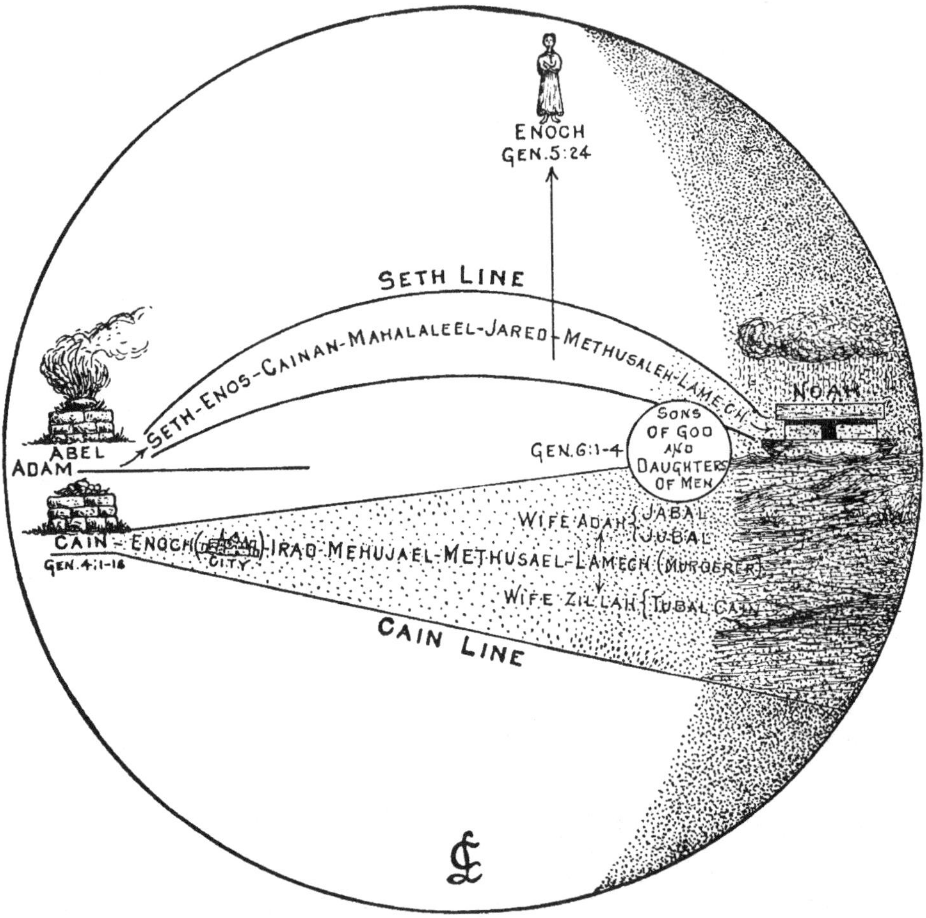

2. ANTEDILUVIAN DISPENSATION
(CONSCIENCE)

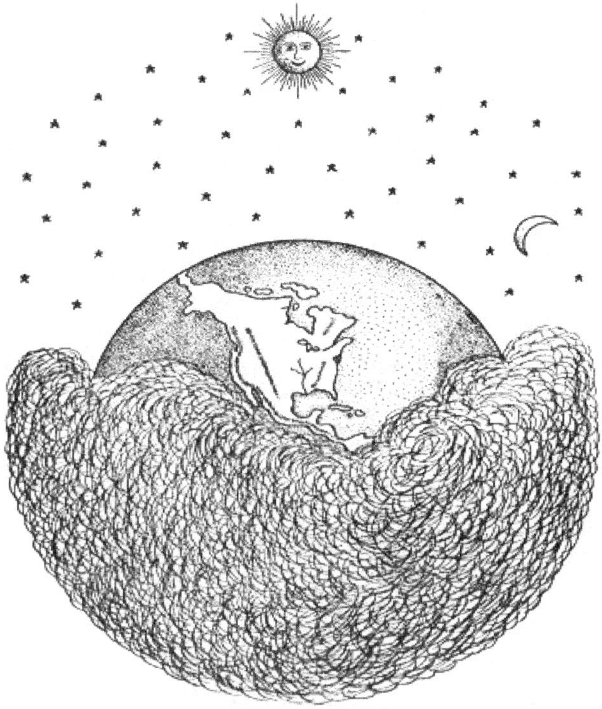

FOURTH DAY
SOLAR LIGHT RESTORED

"KINGDOM OF GOD"-"KINGDOM OF HEAVEN"-"THE CHURCH"

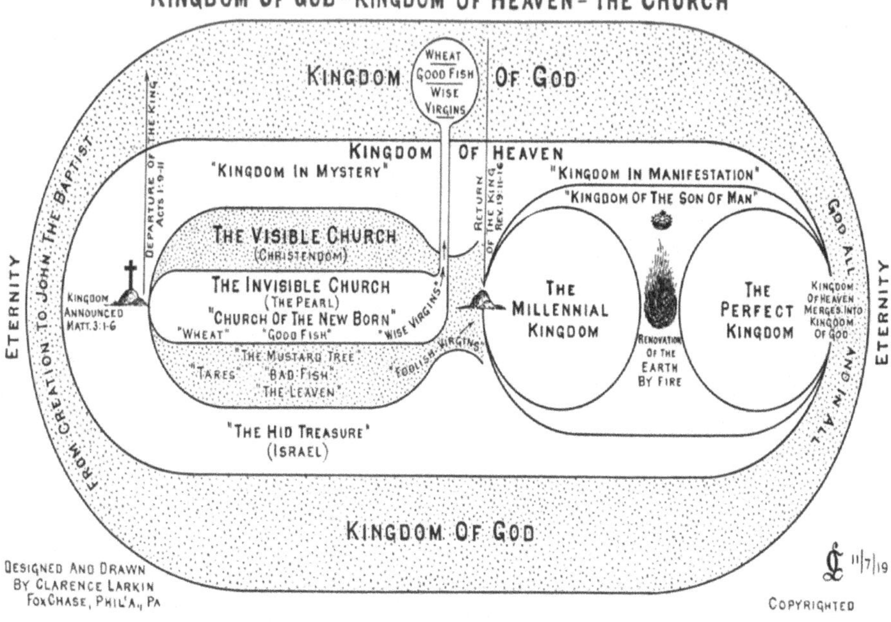

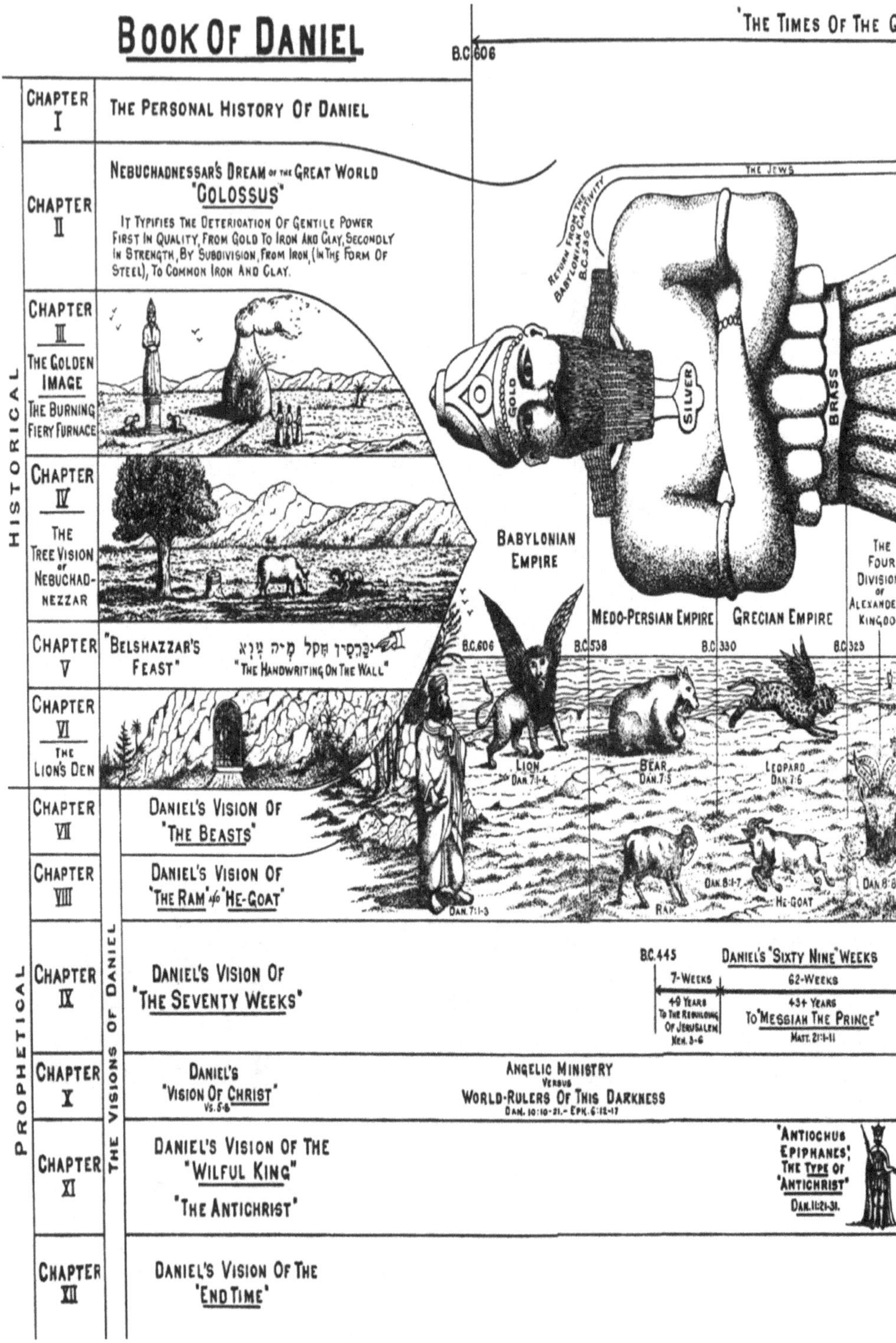
BOOK OF DANIEL
'THE TIMES OF THE G
B.C 606
HISTORICAL
CHAPTER I
THE PERSONAL HISTORY OF DANIEL
CHAPTER II
NEBUCHADNESSAR'S DREAM OF THE GREAT WORLD "COLOSSUS"
IT TYPIFIES THE DETERIORATION OF GENTILE POWER FIRST IN QUALITY, FROM GOLD TO IRON AND CLAY, SECONDLY IN STRENGTH, BY SUBDIVISION, FROM IRON, (IN THE FORM OF STEEL), TO COMMON IRON AND CLAY.
CHAPTER III
THE GOLDEN IMAGE
THE BURNING FIERY FURNACE
CHAPTER IV
THE TREE VISION OF NEBUCHADNEZZAR
CHAPTER V
"BELSHAZZAR'S FEAST"
"THE HANDWRITING ON THE WALL"
CHAPTER VI
THE LION'S DEN
THE JEWS
RETURN FROM THE BABYLONIAN CAPTIVITY B.C.536
GOLD
SILVER
BRASS
BABYLONIAN EMPIRE
MEDO-PERSIAN EMPIRE
GRECIAN EMPIRE
THE FOUR DIVISION OF ALEXANDEF KINGDOM
B.C.606
B.C 538
B.C 330
B.C 323
LION DAN.7:1-4
BEAR DAN.7:5
LEOPARD DAN.7:6
DAN.7:1-3
RAM
HE-GOAT
DAN.8:1-7
DAN.8:8
PROPHETICAL
THE VISIONS OF DANIEL
CHAPTER VII
DANIEL'S VISION OF "THE BEASTS"
CHAPTER VIII
DANIEL'S VISION OF "THE RAM" AND "HE-GOAT"
CHAPTER IX
DANIEL'S VISION OF "THE SEVENTY WEEKS"
B.C.445
DANIEL'S "SIXTY NINE" WEEKS
7-WEEKS
62-WEEKS
49 YEARS TO THE REBUILDING OF JERUSALEM NEH. 3-6
434 YEARS TO "MESSIAH THE PRINCE" MATT. 21:1-11
CHAPTER X
DANIEL'S "VISION OF CHRIST" VS. 5-6
ANGELIC MINISTRY VERSUS WORLD-RULERS OF THIS DARKNESS
DAN. 10:10-21.- EPH. 6:12-17
CHAPTER XI
DANIEL'S VISION OF THE "WILFUL KING"
"THE ANTICHRIST"
"ANTIOCHUS EPIPHANES", THE TYPE OF "ANTICHRIST"
DAN. 11:21-31.
CHAPTER XII
DANIEL'S VISION OF THE "END TIME"

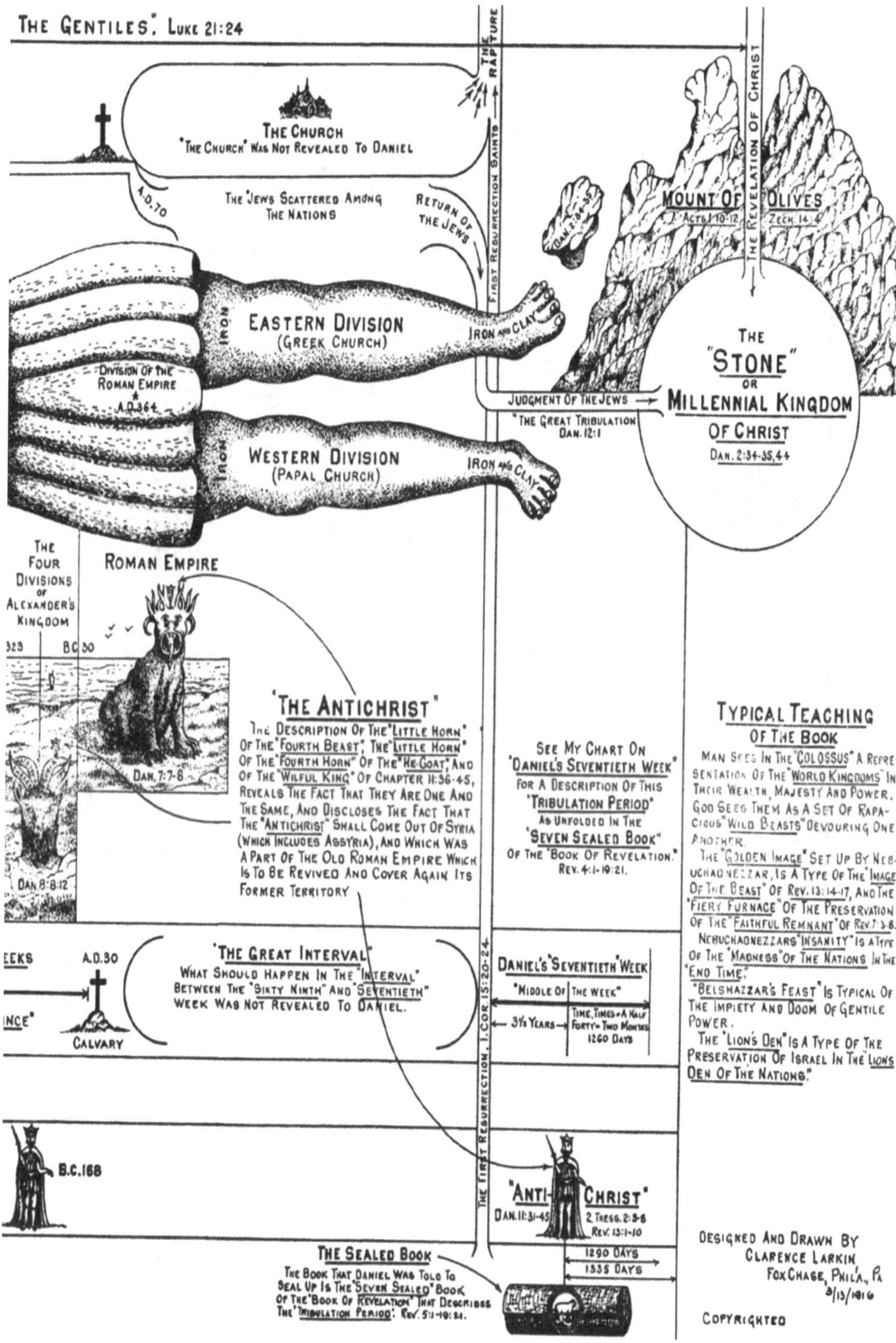
THE GENTILES". LUKE 21:24
THE RAPTURE
THE CHURCH
"THE CHURCH" WAS NOT REVEALED TO DANIEL
A.D.70
THE "JEWS SCATTERED AMONG THE NATIONS
RETURN OF THE JEWS
FIRST RESURRECTION SAINTS
THE REVELATION OF CHRIST
MOUNT OF OLIVES
ACTS 1:10-12
ZECH. 14:4
DAN. 2:34-35
IRON
EASTERN DIVISION
(GREEK CHURCH)
IRON AND CLAY
DIVISION OF THE ROMAN EMPIRE
A.D.364
JUDGMENT OF THE JEWS
"THE GREAT TRIBULATION
DAN. 12:1
THE "STONE" OR MILLENNIAL KINGDOM OF CHRIST
DAN. 2:34-35,44
WESTERN DIVISION
(PAPAL CHURCH)
IRON AND CLAY
THE FOUR DIVISIONS OF ALEXANDER'S KINGDOM
ROMAN EMPIRE
323
BC 30
DAN. 7:7-8
DAN. 8:8-12
"THE ANTICHRIST"
THE DESCRIPTION OF THE "LITTLE HORN" OF THE "FOURTH BEAST", THE "LITTLE HORN" OF THE "FOURTH HORN" OF THE "HE-GOAT", AND OF THE "WILFUL KING" OF CHAPTER 11:36-45, REVEALS THE FACT THAT THEY ARE ONE AND THE SAME, AND DISCLOSES THE FACT THAT THE "ANTICHRIST" SHALL COME OUT OF SYRIA (WHICH INCLUDES ASSYRIA), AND WHICH WAS A PART OF THE OLD ROMAN EMPIRE WHICH IS TO BE REVIVED AND COVER AGAIN ITS FORMER TERRITORY
SEE MY CHART ON "DANIEL'S SEVENTIETH WEEK" FOR A DESCRIPTION OF THIS "TRIBULATION PERIOD" AS UNFOLDED IN THE "SEVEN SEALED BOOK" OF THE "BOOK OF REVELATION." REV. 4:1-19:21.
TYPICAL TEACHING OF THE BOOK
MAN SEES IN THE "COLOSSUS" A REPRESENTATION OF THE "WORLD KINGDOMS" IN THEIR WEALTH, MAJESTY AND POWER. GOD SEES THEM AS A SET OF RAPACIOUS "WILD BEASTS" DEVOURING ONE ANOTHER.
THE "GOLDEN IMAGE" SET UP BY NEBUCHADNEZZAR, IS A TYPE OF THE "IMAGE OF THE BEAST" OF REV. 13:14-17, AND THE "FIERY FURNACE" OF THE PRESERVATION OF THE "FAITHFUL REMNANT" OF REV. 7:3-8.
NEBUCHADNEZZAR'S "INSANITY" IS A TYPE OF THE "MADNESS" OF THE NATIONS IN THE "END TIME."
"BELSHAZZAR'S FEAST" IS TYPICAL OF THE IMPIETY AND DOOM OF GENTILE POWER.
THE "LION'S DEN" IS A TYPE OF THE PRESERVATION OF ISRAEL IN THE "LIONS DEN OF THE NATIONS."
EEKS
A.D.30
INCE"
CALVARY
"THE GREAT INTERVAL"
WHAT SHOULD HAPPEN IN THE "INTERVAL" BETWEEN THE "SIXTY NINTH" AND "SEVENTIETH" WEEK WAS NOT REVEALED TO DANIEL.
THE FIRST RESURRECTION. 1. COR. 15:20-24.
DANIEL'S "SEVENTIETH" WEEK
"MIDDLE OF THE WEEK"
3½ YEARS
TIME, TIMES & A HALF
FORTY-TWO MONTHS
1260 DAYS
B.C.168
"ANTI-CHRIST"
DAN. 11:31-45
2 THESS. 2:3-8
REV. 13:1-10
1290 DAYS
1335 DAYS
THE SEALED BOOK
THE BOOK THAT DANIEL WAS TOLD TO SEAL UP IS THE "SEVEN SEALED" BOOK OF THE "BOOK OF REVELATION" THAT DESCRIBES THE "TRIBULATION PERIOD". REV. 5:1-19:21.
DESIGNED AND DRAWN BY CLARENCE LARKIN FOX CHASE, PHIL'A., PA
3/13/1916
COPYRIGHTED

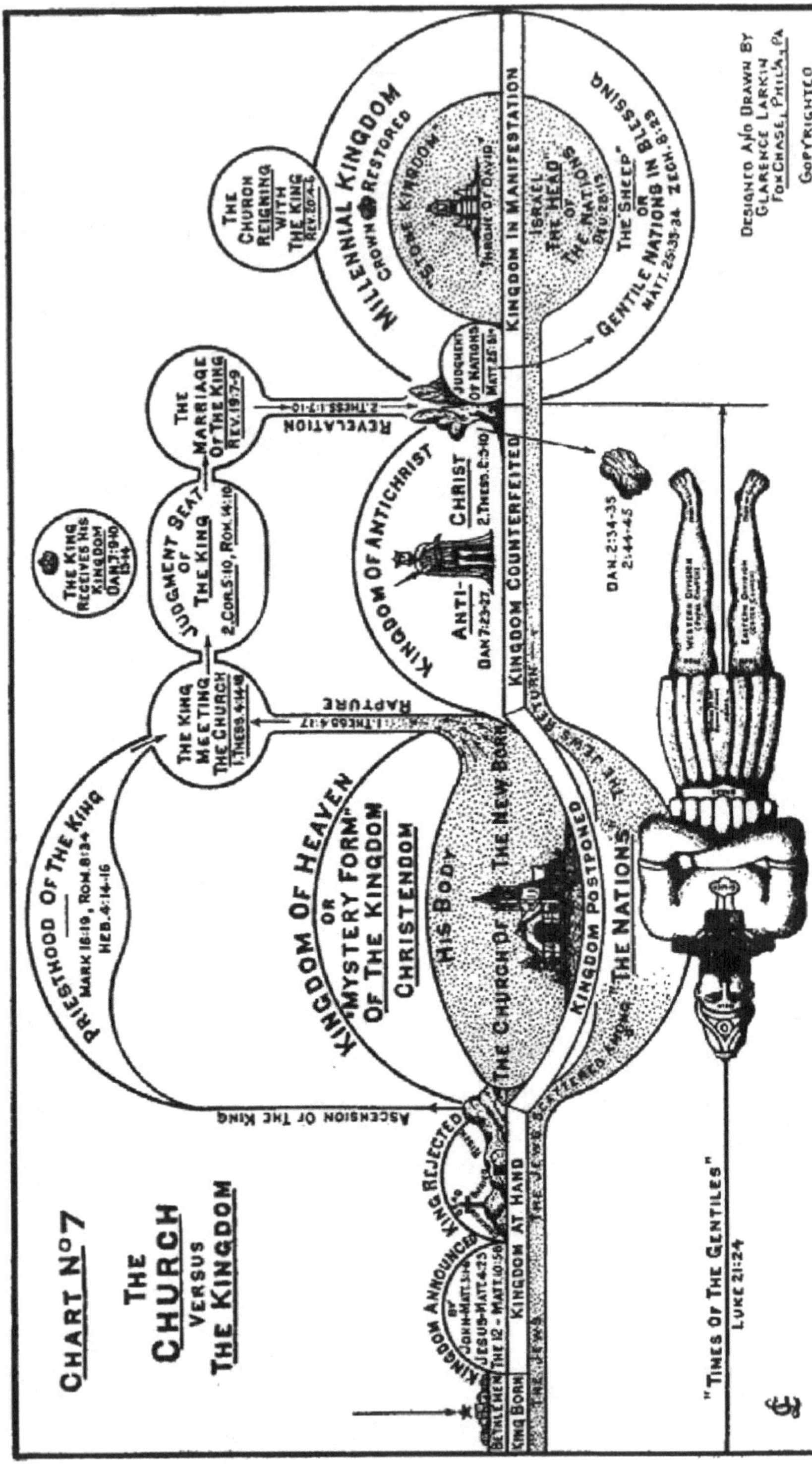
CHART No 7
THE CHURCH VERSUS THE KINGDOM
KINGDOM ANNOUNCED BY JOHN-MATT.3:1-2 JESUS-MATT.4:23 THE 12-MATT.10:5-6
KING REJECTED
ASCENSION OF THE KING
PRIESTHOOD OF THE KING MARK 16:19, ROM.8:34 HEB.4:14-16
THE KING MEETING THE CHURCH 1.THESS.4:14-18
RAPTURE
1.THESS.4:17
KINGDOM OF HEAVEN OR "MYSTERY FORM" OF THE KINGDOM CHRISTENDOM
HIS BODY
THE CHURCH OF THE NEW BORN
KINGDOM POSTPONED
"THE NATIONS"
THE JEWS RETURN
THE JEWS SCATTERED AMONG
BETHLEHEM
KING BORN
KINGDOM AT HAND
THE JEWS
THE KING RECEIVES HIS KINGDOM DAN.7:9-10 13-14
JUDGMENT SEAT OF THE KING 2.COR.5:10, ROM.14:10
THE MARRIAGE OF THE KING REV.19:7-9
REVELATION
2.THESS.1:7-10
KINGDOM OF ANTICHRIST
ANTI-CHRIST DAN.7:23-27 2.THESS.2:3-10
KINGDOM COUNTERFEITED
DAN.2:34-35 2:44-45
THE CHURCH REIGNING WITH THE KING REV.20:4-6
MILLENNIAL KINGDOM CROWN RESTORED
"STONE KINGDOM"
THRONE OF DAVID
ISRAEL THE HEAD OF THE NATIONS DEU.28:13
JUDGMENT OF NATIONS MATT.25:31+
KINGDOM IN MANIFESTATION
GENTILE NATIONS IN BLESSING
THE "SHEEP" OR GENTILE NATIONS IN BLESSING MATT.25:33-34 ZECH.8:23
"TIMES OF THE GENTILES" LUKE 21:24
DESIGNED AND DRAWN BY CLARENCE LARKIN FOX CHASE, PHILA., PA
COPYRIGHTED

FLESH OF BIRDS, BEASTS, MEN AND FISHES
BODIES CELESTIAL AND TERRESTRIAL

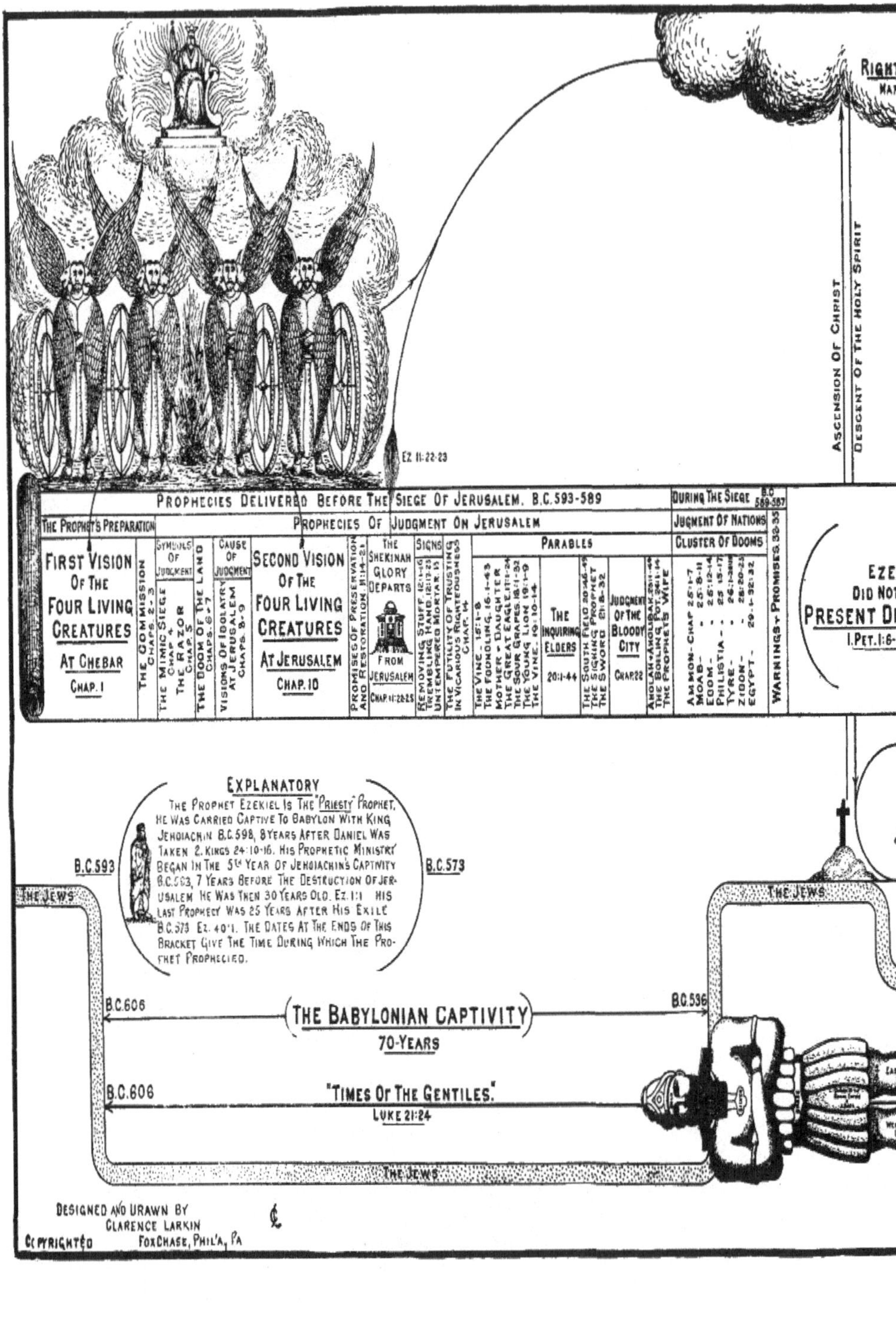

EZ 11:22-23
Prophecies Delivered Before The Siege Of Jerusalem. B.C.593-589
During The Siege B.C. 589-587
The Prophet's Preparation
Prophecies Of Judgment On Jerusalem
Jugment Of Nations
Cluster Of Dooms
First Vision Of The Four Living Creatures At Chebar Chap. 1
The Commission Chaps. 2-3
Symbols Of Judgment
The Mimic Siege Chap. 4
The Razor Chap. 5
The Doom Of The Land Chaps. 6-7
Cause Of Judgment
Visions Of Idolatry At Jerusalem Chaps. 8-9
Second Vision Of The Four Living Creatures At Jerusalem Chap. 10
Promises Of Preservation And Restoration 11:14-21
The Shekinah Glory Departs From Jerusalem Chap. 11:22-25
Signs
Parables
The Inquiring Elders 20:1-44
Judgment Of The Bloody City Chap. 22
Warnings & Promises 33-35
Ascension Of Christ
Descent Of The Holy Spirit
Explanatory
The Prophet Ezekiel Is The "Priesty" Prophet. He Was Carried Captive To Babylon With King Jehoiachin B.C.598, 8 Years After Daniel Was Taken 2. Kings 24:10-16. His Prophetic Ministry Began In The 5th Year Of Jehoiachin's Captivity B.C.593, 7 Years Before The Destruction Of Jerusalem He Was Then 30 Years Old. Ez. 1:1 His Last Prophecy Was 25 Years After His Exile B.C.573 Ez. 40:1. The Dates At The Ends Of This Bracket Give The Time During Which The Prophet Prophecied.
B.C.593
B.C.573
The Jews
B.C.606
The Babylonian Captivity
70-Years
B.C.536
B.C.606
"Times Of The Gentiles."
Luke 21:24
The Jews
The Jews
Designed And Drawn By
Clarence Larkin
Fox Chase, Phil'a, Pa
Copyrighted

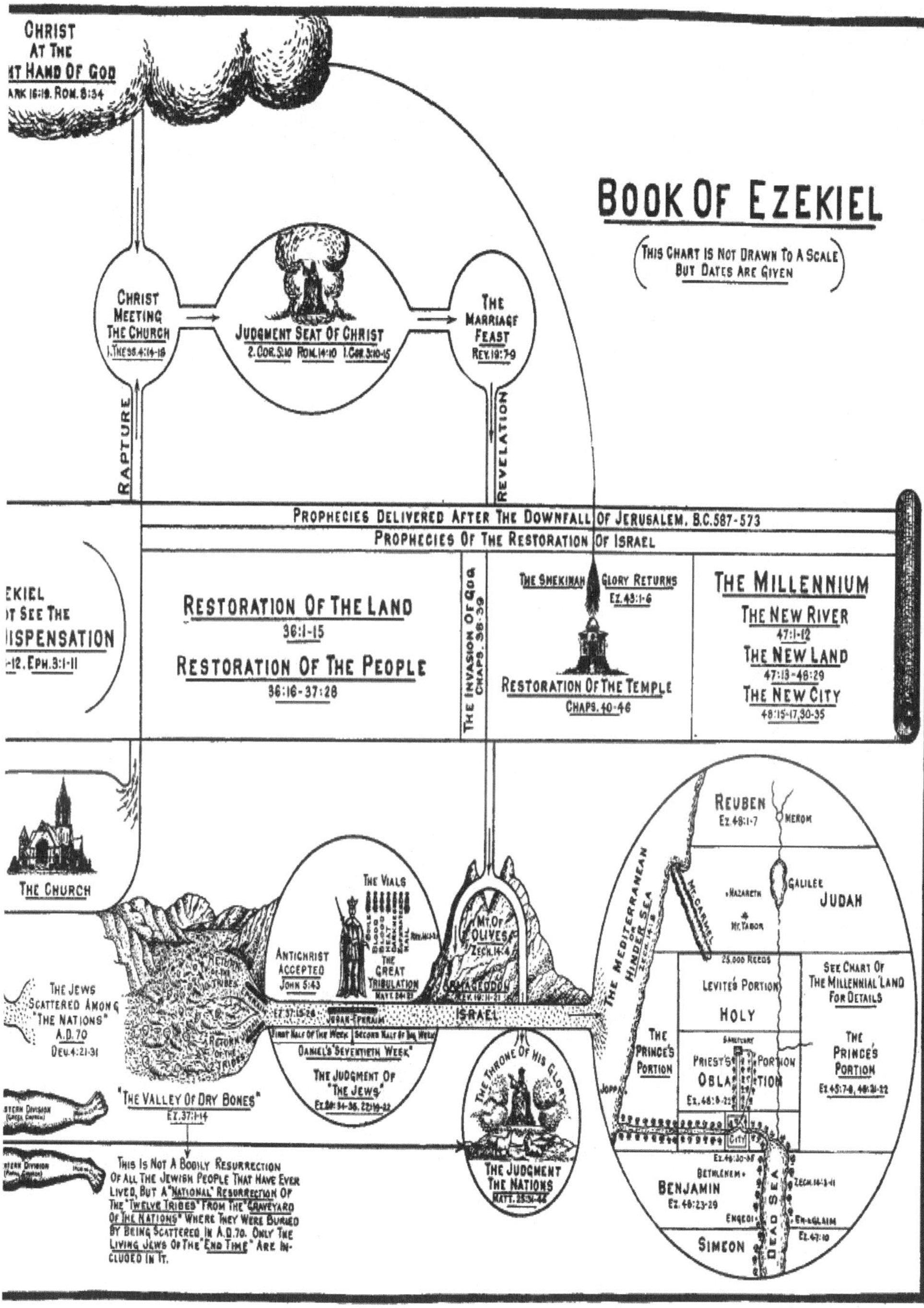
CHRIST
AT THE
HAND OF GOD
ARK 16:19. ROM. 8:34
BOOK OF EZEKIEL
(THIS CHART IS NOT DRAWN TO A SCALE BUT DATES ARE GIVEN)
CHRIST MEETING THE CHURCH
I.THESS.4:14-16
JUDGMENT SEAT OF CHRIST
2.COR.5:10 ROM.14:10 1.COR.3:10-15
THE MARRIAGE FEAST
REV.19:7-9
RAPTURE
REVELATION
PROPHECIES DELIVERED AFTER THE DOWNFALL OF JERUSALEM, B.C.587-573
PROPHECIES OF THE RESTORATION OF ISRAEL
EKIEL
T SEE THE
ISPENSATION
-12. EPH.3:1-11
RESTORATION OF THE LAND
36:1-15
RESTORATION OF THE PEOPLE
36:16-37:28
THE INVASION OF GOG
CHAPS. 38-39
THE SHEKINAH GLORY RETURNS
EZ.43:1-6
RESTORATION OF THE TEMPLE
CHAPS. 40-46
THE MILLENNIUM
THE NEW RIVER
47:1-12
THE NEW LAND
47:13-48:29
THE NEW CITY
48:15-17,30-35
THE CHURCH
THE VIALS
ANTICHRIST ACCEPTED
JOHN 5:43
THE GREAT TRIBULATION
MT. OF OLIVES
ZECH.14:4
ARMAGEDDON
REV.19:11-21
THE JEWS SCATTERED AMONG "THE NATIONS" A.D.70
DEU.4:21-31
RETURN OF THE TRIBES
EZ.37:15-28
JUDAH-EPHRAIM
ISRAEL
FIRST HALF OF THE WEEK
SECOND HALF OF THE WEEK
DANIEL'S SEVENTIETH WEEK
THE JUDGMENT OF "THE JEWS"
"THE VALLEY OF DRY BONES"
EZ.37:1-14
THE THRONE OF HIS GLORY
THE JUDGMENT THE NATIONS
MATT.25:31-46
THIS IS NOT A BODILY RESURRECTION OF ALL THE JEWISH PEOPLE THAT HAVE EVER LIVED, BUT A "NATIONAL" RESURRECTION OF THE "TWELVE TRIBES" FROM THE "GRAVEYARD OF THE NATIONS" WHERE THEY WERE BURIED BY BEING SCATTERED IN A.D.70. ONLY THE LIVING JEWS OF THE "END TIME" ARE INCLUDED IN IT.
THE MEDITERRANEAN OR HINDER SEA
MT. CARMEL
REUBEN
EZ.48:1-7
MEROM
NAZARETH
MT. TABOR
GALILEE
JUDAH
25,000 REEDS
SEE CHART OF THE MILLENNIAL LAND FOR DETAILS
LEVITE'S PORTION
HOLY
THE PRINCE'S PORTION
PRIEST'S PORTION
OBLATION
SANCTUARY
JOPPA
CITY
BETHLEHEM
BENJAMIN
EZ.48:23-29
ENGEDI
DEAD SEA
EN-EGLAIM
EZ.47:10
SIMEON

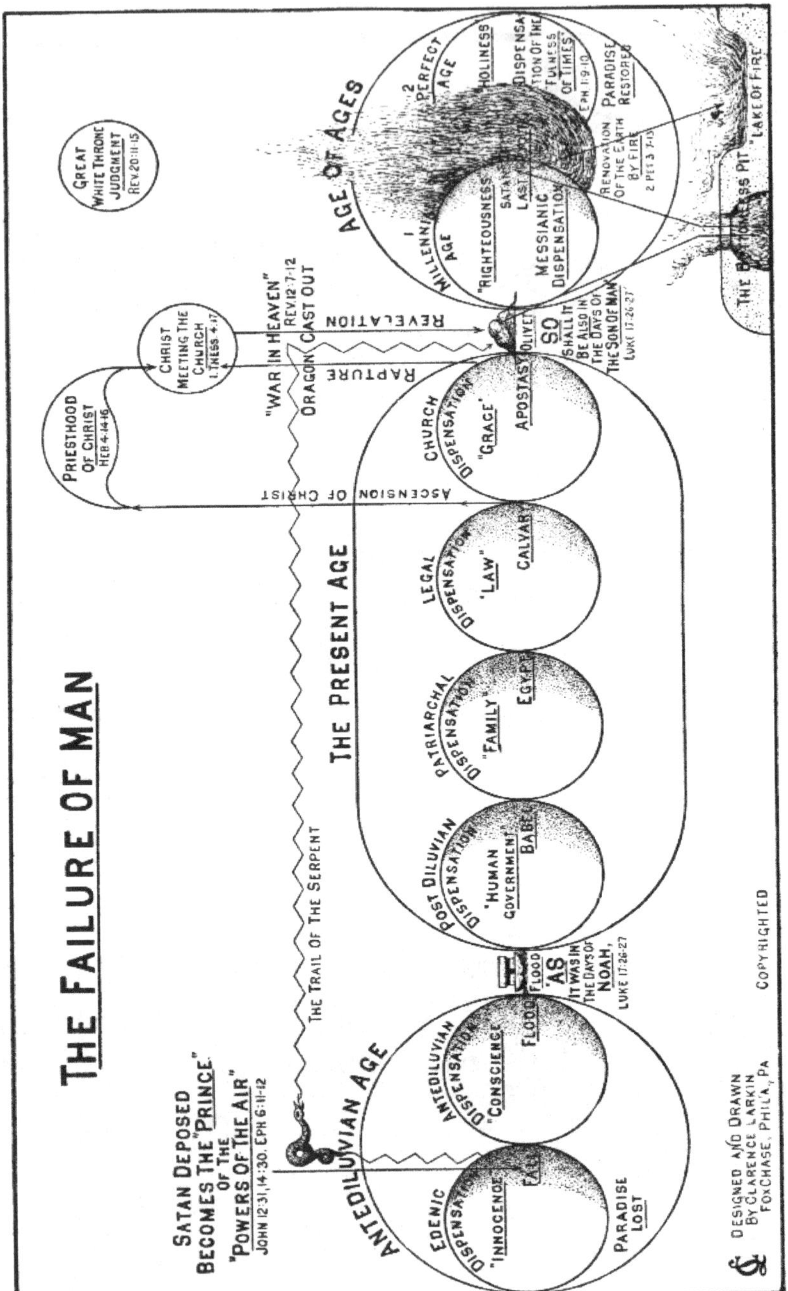
THE FAILURE OF MAN
SATAN DEPOSED BECOMES THE "PRINCE" OF THE "POWERS OF THE AIR" JOHN 12:31, 14:30. EPH 6:11-12
GREAT WHITE THRONE JUDGMENT REV. 20:11-15
PRIESTHOOD OF CHRIST HEB 4:14-16
CHRIST MEETING THE CHURCH 1 THESS. 4:17
"WAR IN HEAVEN" REV. 12:7-12
DRAGON CAST OUT
THE TRAIL OF THE SERPENT
ASCENSION OF CHRIST
RAPTURE
REVELATION
ANTEDILUVIAN AGE
THE PRESENT AGE
AGE OF AGES
EDENIC DISPENSATION "INNOCENCE"
FALL
PARADISE LOST
ANTEDILUVIAN DISPENSATION "CONSCIENCE"
FLOOD
"AS IT WAS IN THE DAYS OF NOAH," LUKE 17:26-27
POST DILUVIAN DISPENSATION "HUMAN GOVERNMENT"
BABEL
PATRIARCHAL DISPENSATION "FAMILY"
EGYPT
LEGAL DISPENSATION "LAW"
CALVARY
CHURCH DISPENSATION "GRACE"
APOSTASY
OLIVET
SO SHALL IT BE ALSO IN THE DAYS OF THE SON OF MAN LUKE 17:26-27
1 MILLENNIAL AGE
"RIGHTEOUSNESS"
MESSIANIC DISPENSATION
2 PERFECT AGE
HOLINESS
DISPENSATION OF THE "FULNESS OF TIMES" EPH. 1:9-10
RENOVATION OF THE EARTH BY FIRE 2 PET. 3:7-13
PARADISE RESTORED
"LAKE OF FIRE"
DESIGNED AND DRAWN BY CLARENCE LARKIN FOX CHASE, PHILA., PA
COPYRIGHTED

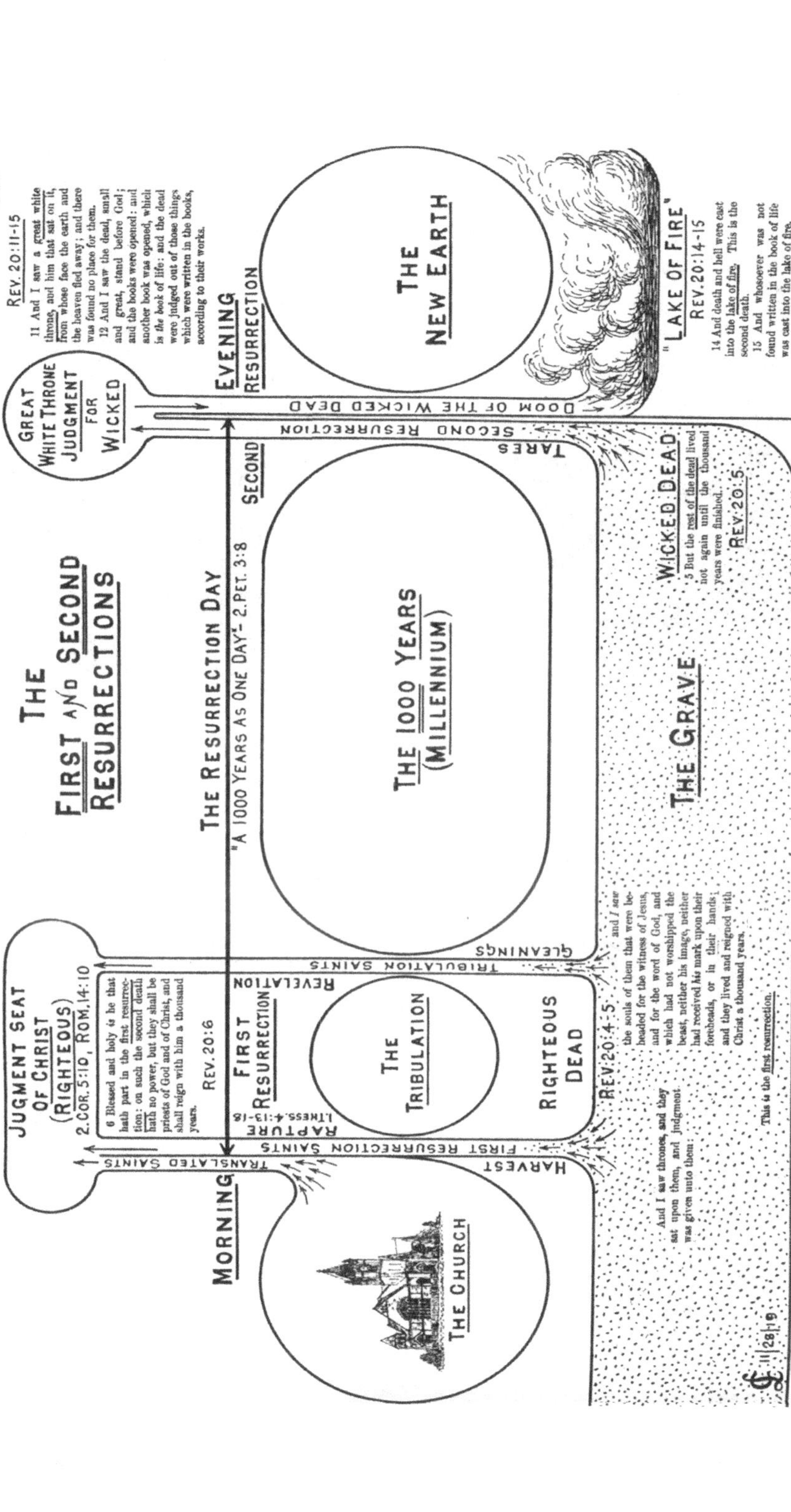
THE FIRST AND SECOND RESURRECTIONS
THE RESURRECTION DAY
"A 1000 YEARS AS ONE DAY" 2.PET. 3:8
MORNING
EVENING RESURRECTION
FIRST RESURRECTION
SECOND
THE CHURCH
TRANSLATED SAINTS
FIRST RESURRECTION SAINTS
HARVEST
JUGMENT SEAT OF CHRIST (RIGHTEOUS) 2.COR. 5:10, ROM. 14:10
6 Blessed and holy is he that hath part in the first resurrection: on such the second death hath no power, but they shall be priests of God and of Christ, and shall reign with him a thousand years.
REV. 20:6
RAPTURE 1.THESS. 4:13-18
REVELATION
THE TRIBULATION
RIGHTEOUS DEAD
TRIBULATION SAINTS
GLEANINGS
REV. 20:4-5
And I saw thrones, and they sat upon them, and judgment was given unto them: and I saw the souls of them that were beheaded for the witness of Jesus, and for the word of God, and which had not worshipped the beast, neither his image, neither had received his mark upon their foreheads, or in their hands; and they lived and reigned with Christ a thousand years.
This is the first resurrection.
THE 1000 YEARS (MILLENNIUM)
THE GRAVE
WICKED DEAD
5 But the rest of the dead lived not again until the thousand years were finished.
REV. 20:5
TARES
SECOND RESURRECTION
GREAT WHITE THRONE JUDGMENT FOR WICKED
DOOM OF THE WICKED DEAD
REV. 20:11-15
11 And I saw a great white throne, and him that sat on it, from whose face the earth and the heaven fled away; and there was found no place for them.
12 And I saw the dead, small and great, stand before God; and the books were opened: and another book was opened, which is the book of life: and the dead were judged out of those things which were written in the books, according to their works.
THE NEW EARTH
"LAKE OF FIRE"
REV. 20:14-15
14 And death and hell were cast into the lake of fire. This is the second death.
15 And whosoever was not found written in the book of life was cast into the lake of fire.
CL 11|28|19

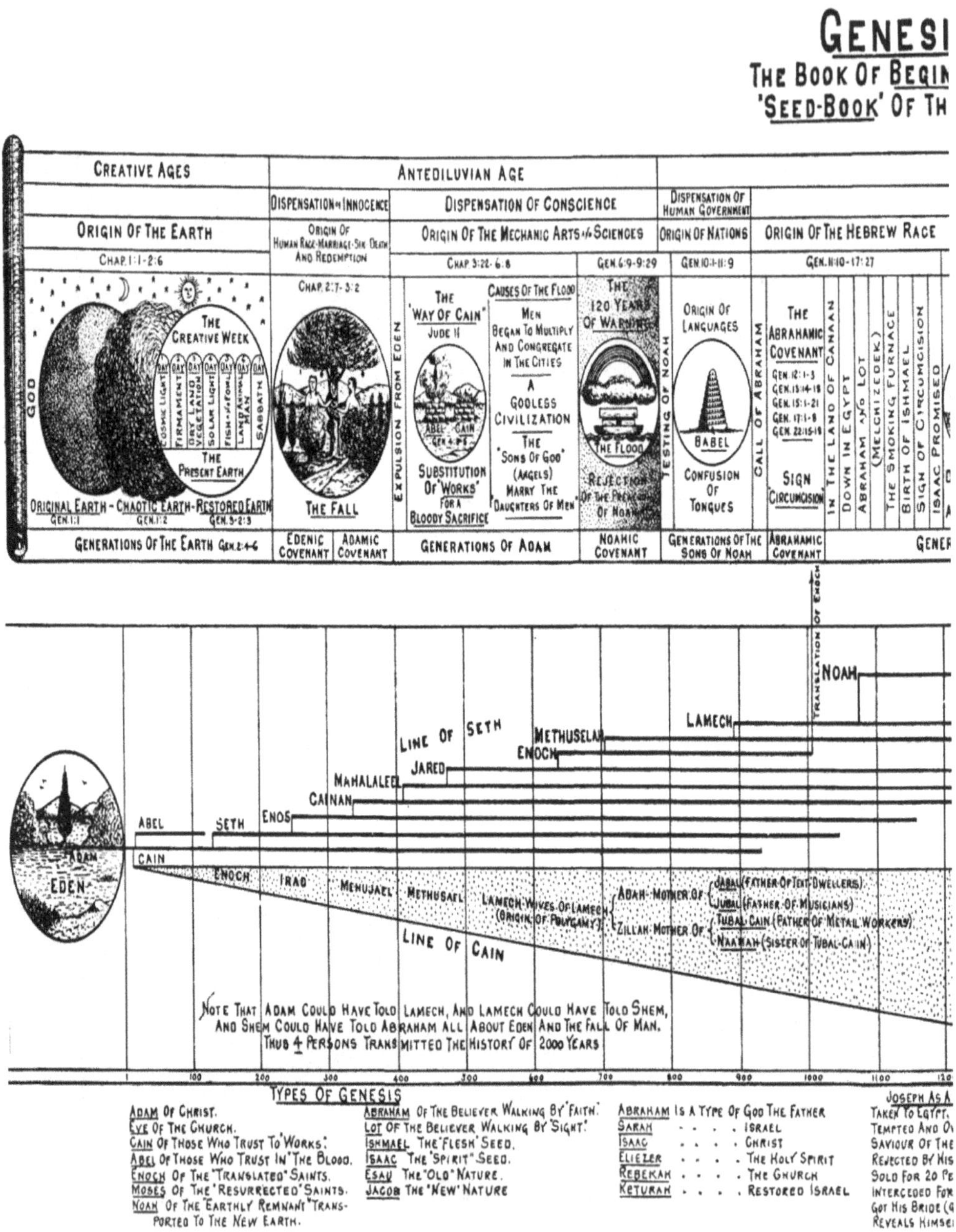
GENESI
THE BOOK OF BEGIN
'SEED-BOOK' OF TH
CREATIVE AGES
ANTEDILUVIAN AGE
DISPENSATION OF INNOCENCE
DISPENSATION OF CONSCIENCE
DISPENSATION OF HUMAN GOVERNMENT
ORIGIN OF THE EARTH
ORIGIN OF HUMAN RACE-MARRIAGE-SIN-DEATH AND REDEMPTION
ORIGIN OF THE MECHANIC ARTS & SCIENCES
ORIGIN OF NATIONS
ORIGIN OF THE HEBREW RACE
CHAP. 1:1-2:6
CHAP. 2:7-3:2
CHAP. 3:22-6:8
GEN. 6:9-9:29
GEN. 10:1-11:9
GEN. 11:10-17:27
GOD
THE CREATIVE WEEK
COSMIC LIGHT
FIRMAMENT
DRY LAND VEGETATION
SOLAR LIGHT
FISH & FOWL
LAND ANIMALS MAN
SABBATH
THE PRESENT EARTH
ORIGINAL EARTH - CHAOTIC EARTH - RESTORED EARTH
GEN. 1:1
GEN. 1:2
GEN. 1:3-2:3
THE FALL
EXPULSION FROM EDEN
THE 'WAY OF CAIN' JUDE 11
ABEL CAIN
SUBSTITUTION OF 'WORKS' FOR A BLOODY SACRIFICE
CAUSES OF THE FLOOD
MEN BEGAN TO MULTIPLY AND CONGREGATE IN THE CITIES
A GODLESS CIVILIZATION
THE 'SONS OF GOD' (ANGELS) MARRY THE DAUGHTERS OF MEN
THE 120 YEARS OF WARNING
THE FLOOD
REJECTION OF THE PREACHING OF NOAH
TESTING OF NOAH
ORIGIN OF LANGUAGES
BABEL
CONFUSION OF TONGUES
CALL OF ABRAHAM
THE ABRAHAMIC COVENANT
GEN. 12:1-3
GEN. 13:14-18
GEN. 15:1-21
GEN. 17:1-9
GEN. 22:15-18
SIGN CIRCUMCISION
IN THE LAND OF CANAAN
DOWN IN EGYPT
ABRAHAM AND LOT
(MELCHIZEDEK)
THE SMOKING FURNACE
BIRTH OF ISHMAEL
SIGN OF CIRCUMCISION
ISAAC PROMISED
GENERATIONS OF THE EARTH GEN. 2:4-6
EDENIC COVENANT
ADAMIC COVENANT
GENERATIONS OF ADAM
NOAHIC COVENANT
GENERATIONS OF THE SONS OF NOAH
ABRAHAMIC COVENANT
GENER
TRANSLATION OF ENOCH
NOAH
LAMECH
METHUSELAH
ENOCH
LINE OF SETH
JARED
MAHALALEEL
CAINAN
ENOS
SETH
ABEL
ADAM
CAIN
EDEN
ENOCH
IRAD
MEHUJAEL
METHUSAEL
LAMECH-WIVES OF LAMECH (ORIGIN OF POLYGAMY)
ADAH-MOTHER OF
ZILLAH-MOTHER OF
JABAL (FATHER OF TENT DWELLERS)
JUBAL (FATHER OF MUSICIANS)
TUBAL-CAIN (FATHER OF METAL WORKERS)
NAAMAH (SISTER OF TUBAL-CAIN)
LINE OF CAIN
NOTE THAT ADAM COULD HAVE TOLD LAMECH, AND LAMECH COULD HAVE TOLD SHEM,
AND SHEM COULD HAVE TOLD ABRAHAM ALL ABOUT EDEN AND THE FALL OF MAN.
THUS 4 PERSONS TRANSMITTED THE HISTORY OF 2000 YEARS
1
100
200
300
400
500
600
700
800
900
1000
1100
120
TYPES OF GENESIS
ADAM OF CHRIST.
EVE OF THE CHURCH.
CAIN OF THOSE WHO TRUST TO 'WORKS'.
ABEL OF THOSE WHO TRUST IN THE BLOOD.
ENOCH OF THE 'TRANSLATED' SAINTS.
MOSES OF THE 'RESURRECTED' SAINTS.
NOAH OF THE 'EARTHLY REMNANT' TRANSPORTED TO THE NEW EARTH.
ABRAHAM OF THE BELIEVER WALKING BY 'FAITH'.
LOT OF THE BELIEVER WALKING BY 'SIGHT'.
ISHMAEL THE 'FLESH' SEED.
ISAAC THE 'SPIRIT' SEED.
ESAU THE 'OLD' NATURE.
JACOB THE 'NEW' NATURE
ABRAHAM IS A TYPE OF GOD THE FATHER
SARAH . . . . ISRAEL
ISAAC . . . . CHRIST
ELIEZER . . . . THE HOLY SPIRIT
REBEKAH . . . . THE CHURCH
KETURAH . . . . RESTORED ISRAEL
JOSEPH AS A
TAKEN TO EGYPT.
TEMPTED AND O
SAVIOUR OF THE
REJECTED BY HIS
SOLD FOR 20 PE
INTERCEDED FOR
GOT HIS BRIDE (G
REVEALS HIMSEL

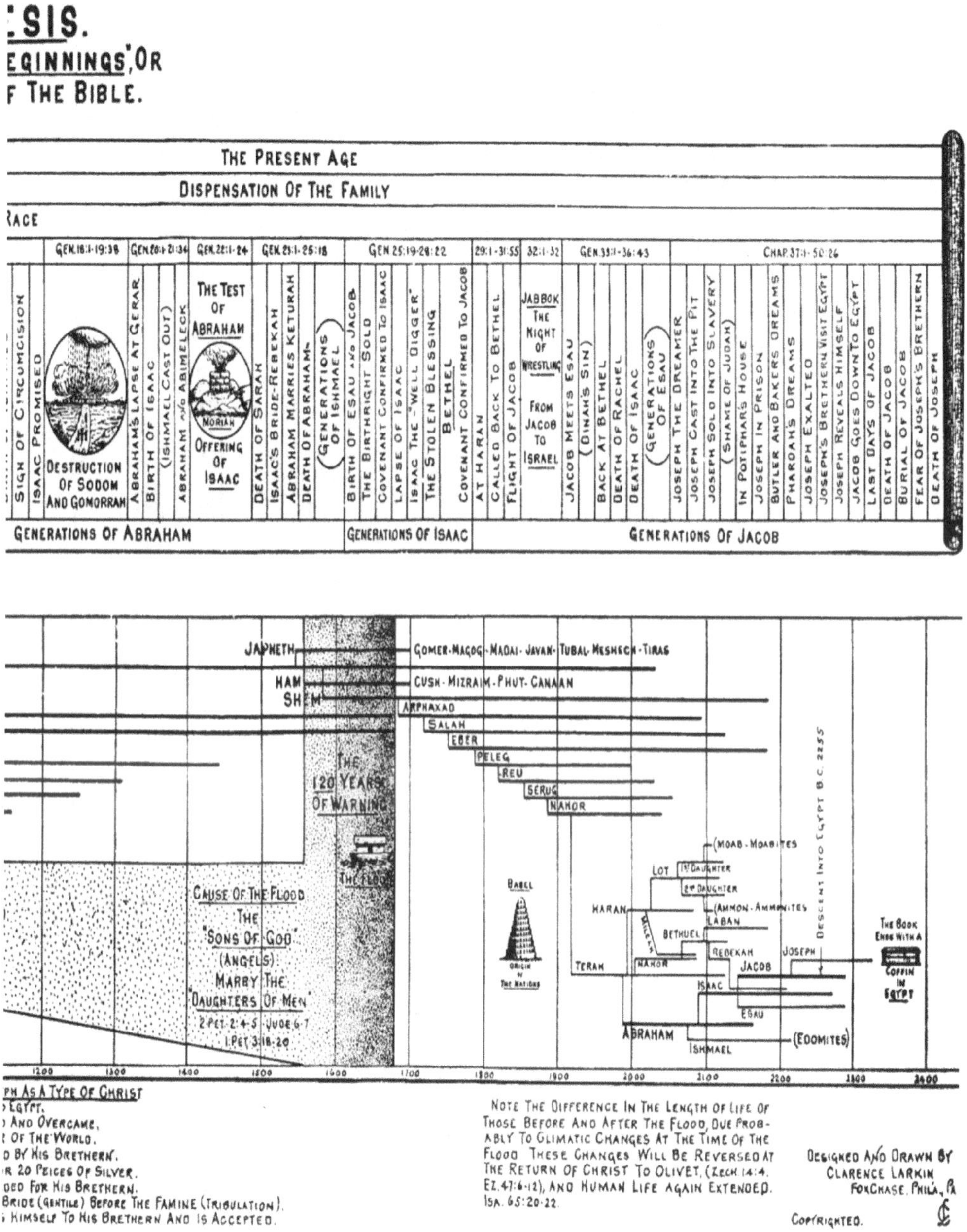

SIS.
EGINNINGS, OR
F THE BIBLE.
THE PRESENT AGE
DISPENSATION OF THE FAMILY
RACE
GEN.18:1-19:38
GEN.20:1-21:34
GEN.22:1-24
GEN.23:1-25:18
GEN 25:19-28:22
29:1-31:55
32:1-32
GEN.33:1-36:43
CHAP.37:1-50:26
SIGN OF CIRCUMCISION
ISAAC PROMISED
DESTRUCTION OF SODOM AND GOMORRAH
ABRAHAM'S LAPSE AT GERAR
BIRTH OF ISAAC
(ISHMAEL CAST OUT)
ABRAHAM AND ABIMELECK
THE TEST OF ABRAHAM
MORIAH
OFFERING OF ISAAC
DEATH OF SARAH
ISAAC'S BRIDE-REBEKAH
ABRAHAM MARRIES KETURAH
DEATH OF ABRAHAM
(GENERATIONS OF ISHMAEL)
BIRTH OF ESAU AND JACOB
THE BIRTHRIGHT SOLD
COVENANT CONFIRMED TO ISAAC
LAPSE OF ISAAC
ISAAC THE "WELL DIGGER"
THE STOLEN BLESSING
BETHEL
COVENANT CONFIRMED TO JACOB
AT HARAN
CALLED BACK TO BETHEL
FLIGHT OF JACOB
JABBOK
THE NIGHT OF WRESTLING
FROM JACOB TO ISRAEL
JACOB MEETS ESAU
(DINAH'S SIN)
BACK AT BETHEL
DEATH OF RACHEL
DEATH OF ISAAC
(GENERATIONS OF ESAU)
JOSEPH THE DREAMER
JOSEPH CAST INTO THE PIT
JOSEPH SOLD INTO SLAVERY
(SHAME OF JUDAH)
IN POTIPHAR'S HOUSE
JOSEPH IN PRISON
BUTLER AND BAKERS DREAMS
PHARAOH'S DREAMS
JOSEPH EXALTED
JOSEPH'S BRETHERN VISIT EGYPT
JOSEPH REVEALS HIMSELF
JACOB GOES DOWN TO EGYPT
LAST DAYS OF JACOB
DEATH OF JACOB
BURIAL OF JACOB
FEAR OF JOSEPH'S BRETHERN
DEATH OF JOSEPH
GENERATIONS OF ABRAHAM
GENERATIONS OF ISAAC
GENERATIONS OF JACOB
JAPHETH
GOMER-MAGOG-MADAI-JAVAN-TUBAL-MESHECH-TIRAS
HAM
CUSH-MIZRAIM-PHUT-CANAAN
SHEM
ARPHAXAD
SALAH
EBER
PELEG
REU
SERUG
NAHOR
THE 120 YEARS OF WARNING
THE FLOOD
CAUSE OF THE FLOOD
THE "SONS OF GOD" (ANGELS) MARRY THE DAUGHTERS OF MEN
2 PET. 2:4-5 JUDE 6-7
1 PET. 3:18-20
BABEL
ORIGIN OF THE NATIONS
(MOAB-MOABITES
LOT
1ST DAUGHTER
2ND DAUGHTER
(AMMON-AMMONITES
HARAN
LABAN
BETHUEL
REBEKAH
JOSEPH
JACOB
NAHOR
TERAH
ISAAC
ESAU
ABRAHAM
ISHMAEL
(EDOMITES)
DESCENT INTO EGYPT B.C. 2255
THE BOOK ENDS WITH A COFFIN IN EGYPT
1200
1300
1400
1500
1600
1700
1800
1900
2000
2100
2200
2300
2400
PH AS A TYPE OF CHRIST
EGYPT.
AND OVERCAME.
OF THE WORLD.
D BY HIS BRETHERN.
R 20 PEICES OF SILVER.
OED FOR HIS BRETHERN.
BRIDE (GENTILE) BEFORE THE FAMINE (TRIBULATION).
HIMSELF TO HIS BRETHERN AND IS ACCEPTED.
NOTE THE DIFFERENCE IN THE LENGTH OF LIFE OF THOSE BEFORE AND AFTER THE FLOOD, DUE PROBABLY TO CLIMATIC CHANGES AT THE TIME OF THE FLOOD. THESE CHANGES WILL BE REVERSED AT THE RETURN OF CHRIST TO OLIVET, (ZECH 14:4. EZ.47:6-12), AND HUMAN LIFE AGAIN EXTENDED. ISA. 65:20-22.
DESIGNED AND DRAWN BY CLARENCE LARKIN FOXCHASE, PHILA, PA
COPYRIGHTED.

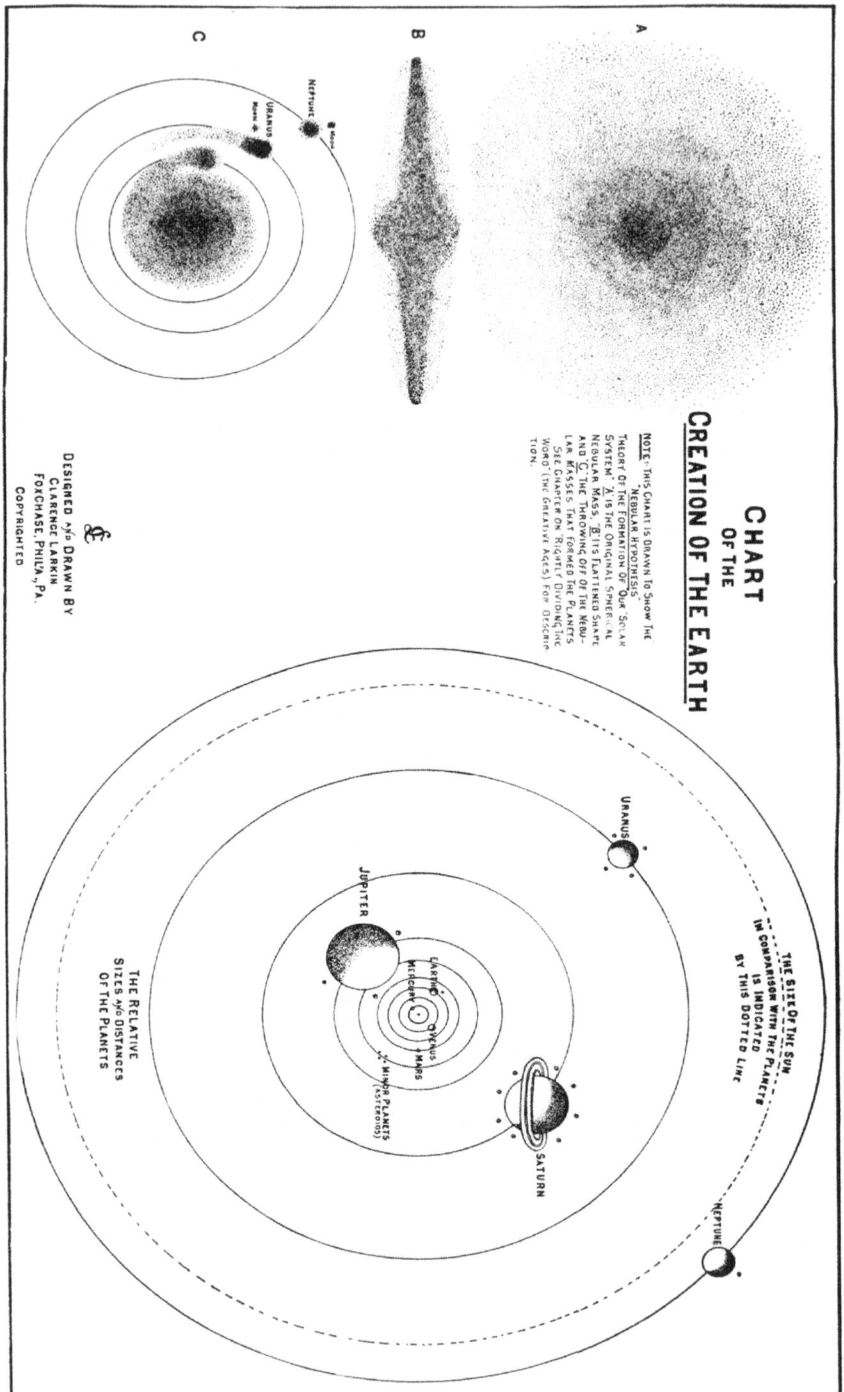
CHART
OF THE
CREATION OF THE EARTH
NOTE:- THIS CHART IS DRAWN TO SHOW THE "NEBULAR HYPOTHESIS" THEORY OF THE FORMATION OF "OUR SOLAR SYSTEM." "A" IS THE ORIGINAL SPHERICAL NEBULAR MASS. "B" ITS FLATTENED SHAPE AND "C" THE THROWING OFF OF THE NEBULAR MASSES THAT FORMED THE PLANETS. SEE CHAPTER ON "RIGHTLY DIVIDING THE WORD" (THE CREATIVE AGES) FOR DESCRIPTION.
A
B
C
NEPTUNE
URANUS
THE SIZE OF THE SUN IN COMPARISON WITH THE PLANETS IS INDICATED BY THIS DOTTED LINE
JUPITER
SATURN
EARTH
MERCURY
VENUS
MARS
MINOR PLANETS (ASTEROIDS)
THE RELATIVE SIZES AND DISTANCES OF THE PLANETS
DESIGNED AND DRAWN BY CLARENCE LARKIN FOXCHASE, PHILA., PA.
COPYRIGHTED

THIRD DAY
TWO WORKS
THE LAND REAPPEARS | VEGETATION REAPPEARS

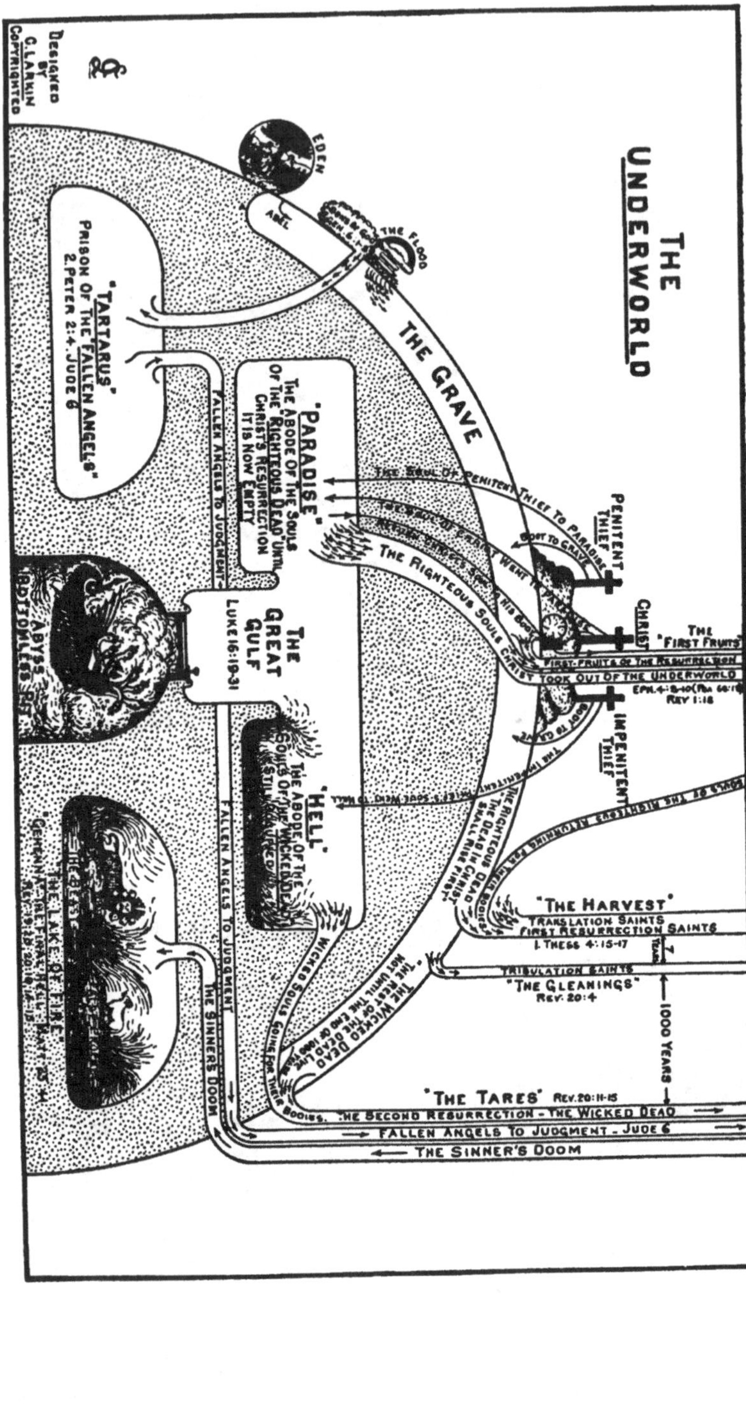
THE UNDERWORLD
EDEN
ABEL
THE FLOOD
THE GRAVE
DESIGNED BY C. LARKIN COPYRIGHTED
"TARTARUS"
PRISON OF THE "FALLEN ANGELS"
2. PETER 2:4. JUDE 6
"PARADISE"
THE ABODE OF THE SOULS OF THE "RIGHTEOUS DEAD" UNTIL CHRISTS RESURRECTION
IT IS NOW EMPTY
FALLEN ANGELS TO JUDGMENT
THE GREAT GULF
LUKE 16:19-31
ABYSS
BOTTOMLESS PIT
"HELL"
THE ABODE OF THE SOULS OF THE WICKED DEAD
THE LAKE OF FIRE
PENITENT THIEF
CHRIST
IMPENITENT THIEF
THE SOUL OF PENITENT THIEF TO PARADISE
BODY TO GRAVE
THE RIGHTEOUS SOULS CHRIST TOOK OUT OF THE UNDERWORLD
"FIRST FRUITS"
FIRST-FRUITS OF THE RESURRECTION
EPH. 4:8-10
REV 1:18
THE RIGHTEOUS DEAD
THE DEAD IN CHRIST SHALL RISE FIRST
"THE HARVEST"
TRANSLATION SAINTS
FIRST RESURRECTION SAINTS
I. THESS 4:15-17
TRIBULATION SAINTS
"THE GLEANINGS"
REV. 20:4
1000 YEARS
THE WICKED DEAD
NOT UNTIL THE REST OF THE DEAD LIVE
WICKED SOULS GOING FOR THEIR BODIES
"THE TARES" REV. 20:11-15
THE SECOND RESURRECTION - THE WICKED DEAD
FALLEN ANGELS TO JUDGMENT - JUDE 6
THE SINNER'S DOOM

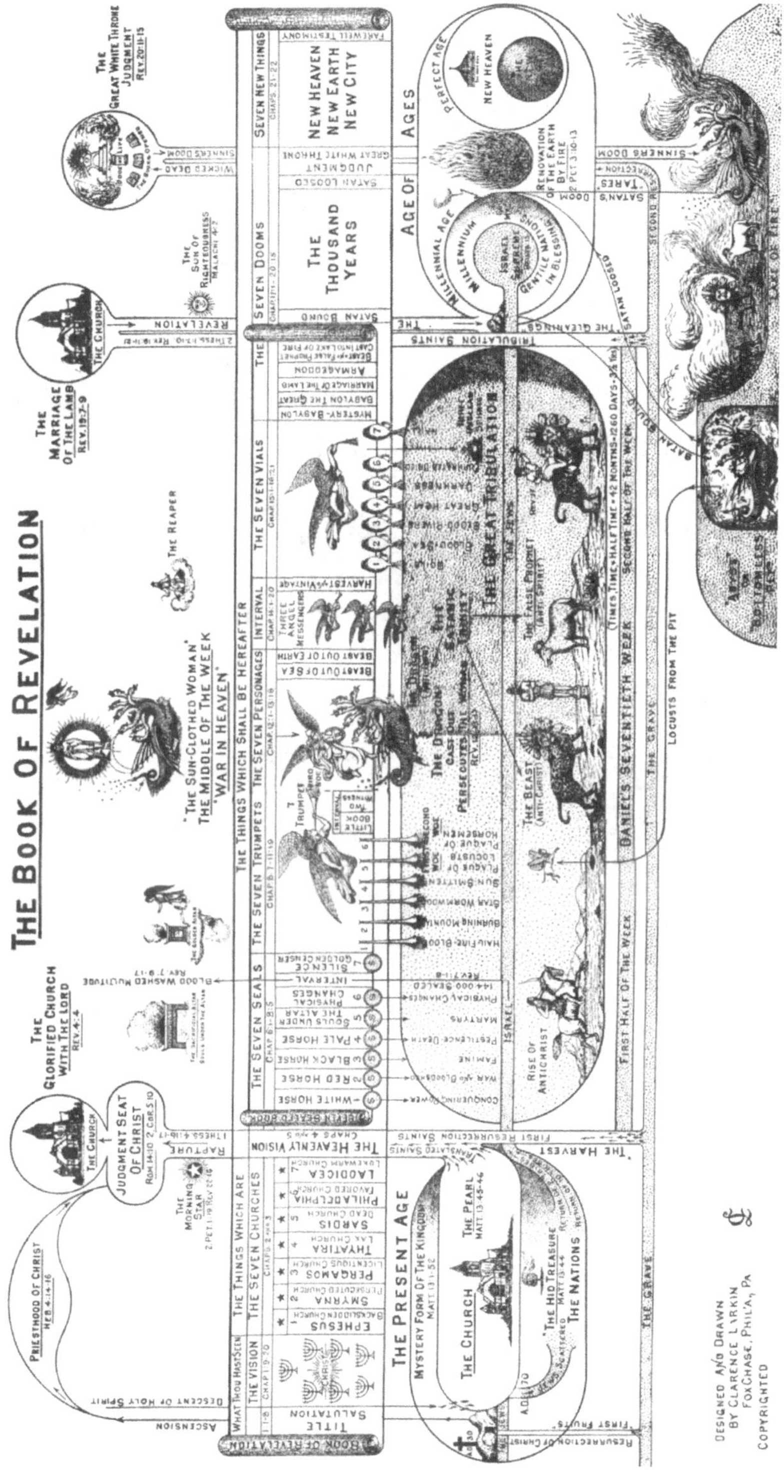
The Book of Revelation
The Things Which Shall Be Hereafter
The Seven Churches
The Seven Seals
The Seven Trumpets
The Seven Personages
The Seven Vials
The Seven Dooms
Seven New Things
New Heaven
New Earth
New City
The Thousand Years
The Present Age
Age of Ages
The Great Tribulation
Daniel's Seventieth Week
First Half of The Week
Second Half of The Week
The Sun-Clothed Woman
The Middle of The Week
War in Heaven
Lake of Fire
Designed and Drawn
by Clarence Larkin
FoxChase, Phila, Pa
Copyrighted

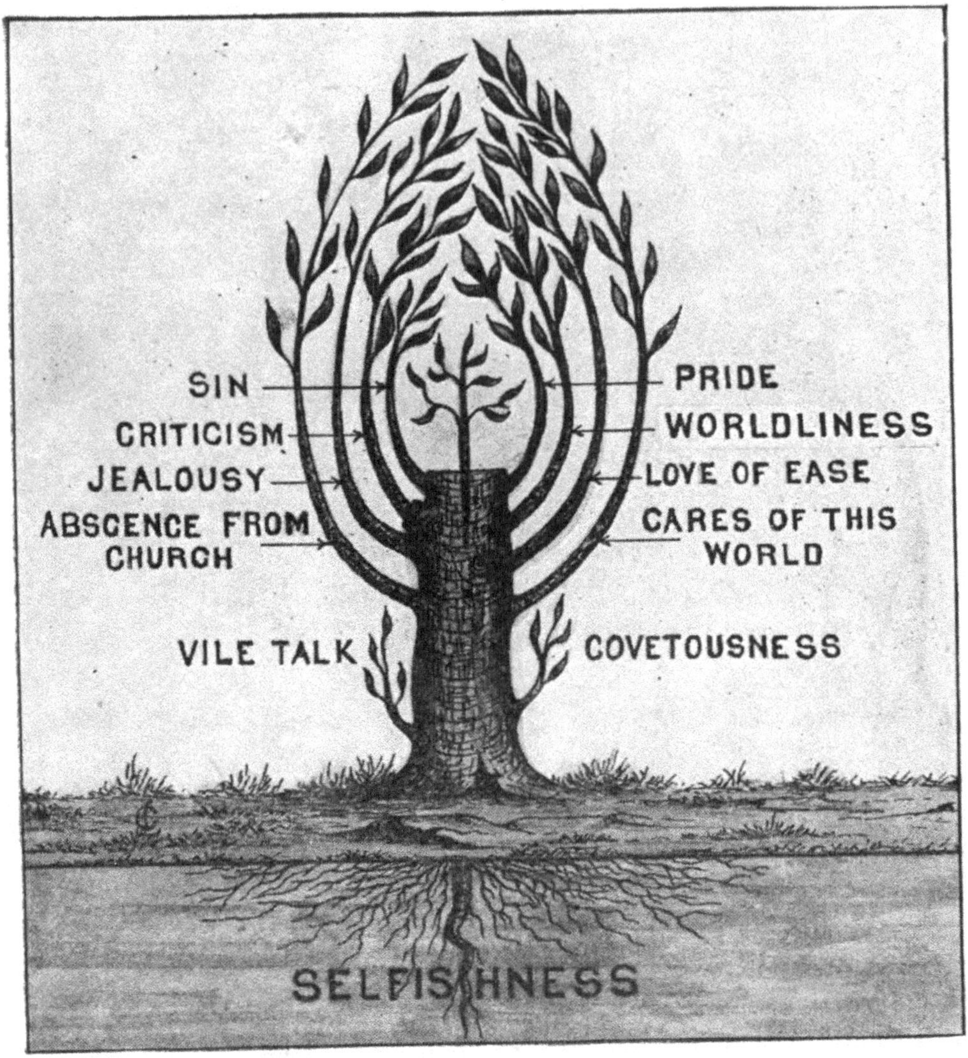
SIN
CRITICISM
JEALOUSY
ABSCENCE FROM CHURCH
PRIDE
WORLDLINESS
LOVE OF EASE
CARES OF THIS WORLD
VILE TALK
COVETOUSNESS
SELFISHNESS

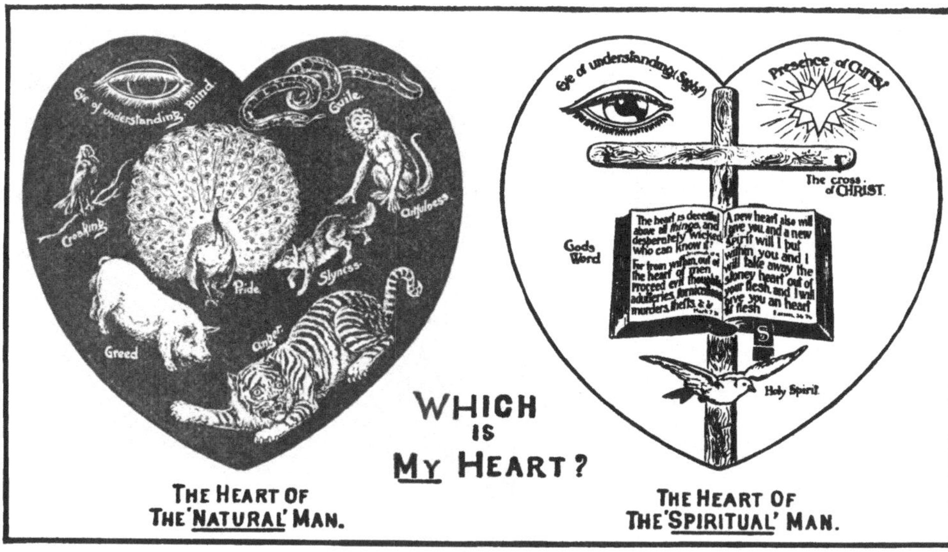

1. EDENIC DISPENSATION
(INNOCENCE)

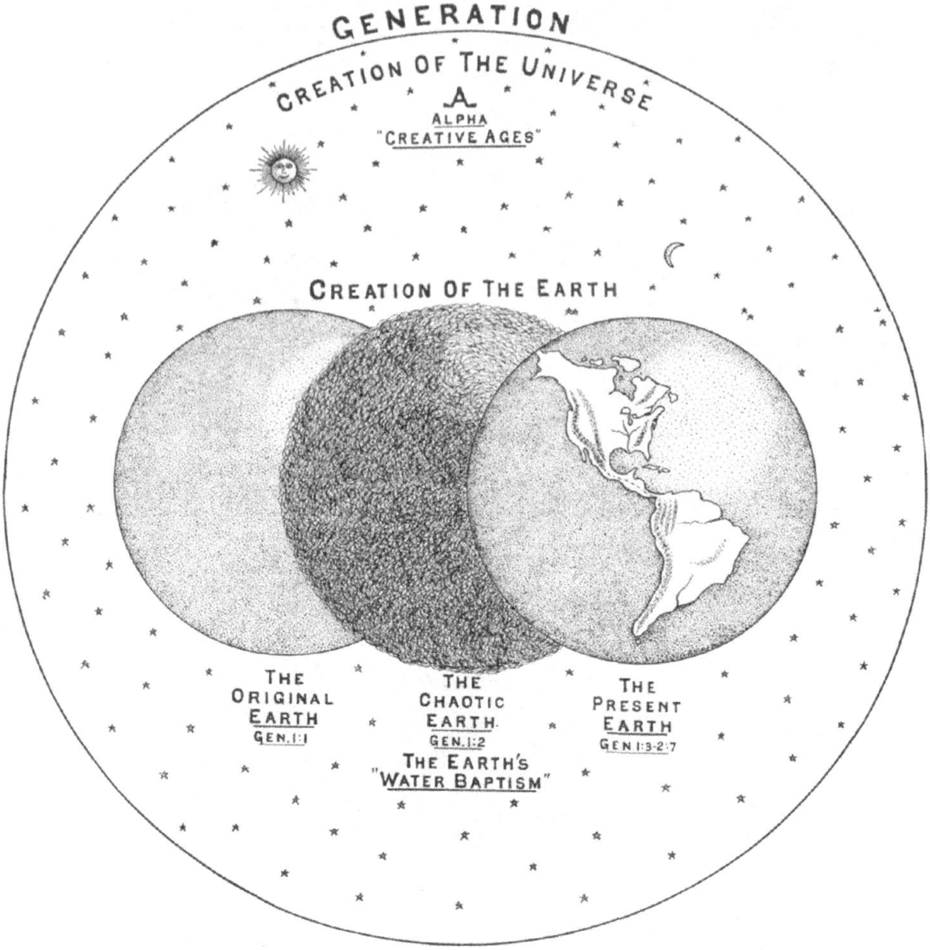
GENERATION
CREATION OF THE UNIVERSE
A
ALPHA
"CREATIVE AGES"
CREATION OF THE EARTH
THE ORIGINAL EARTH
GEN. 1:1
THE CHAOTIC EARTH
GEN. 1:2
THE EARTH'S "WATER BAPTISM"
THE PRESENT EARTH
GEN. 1:3-2:7

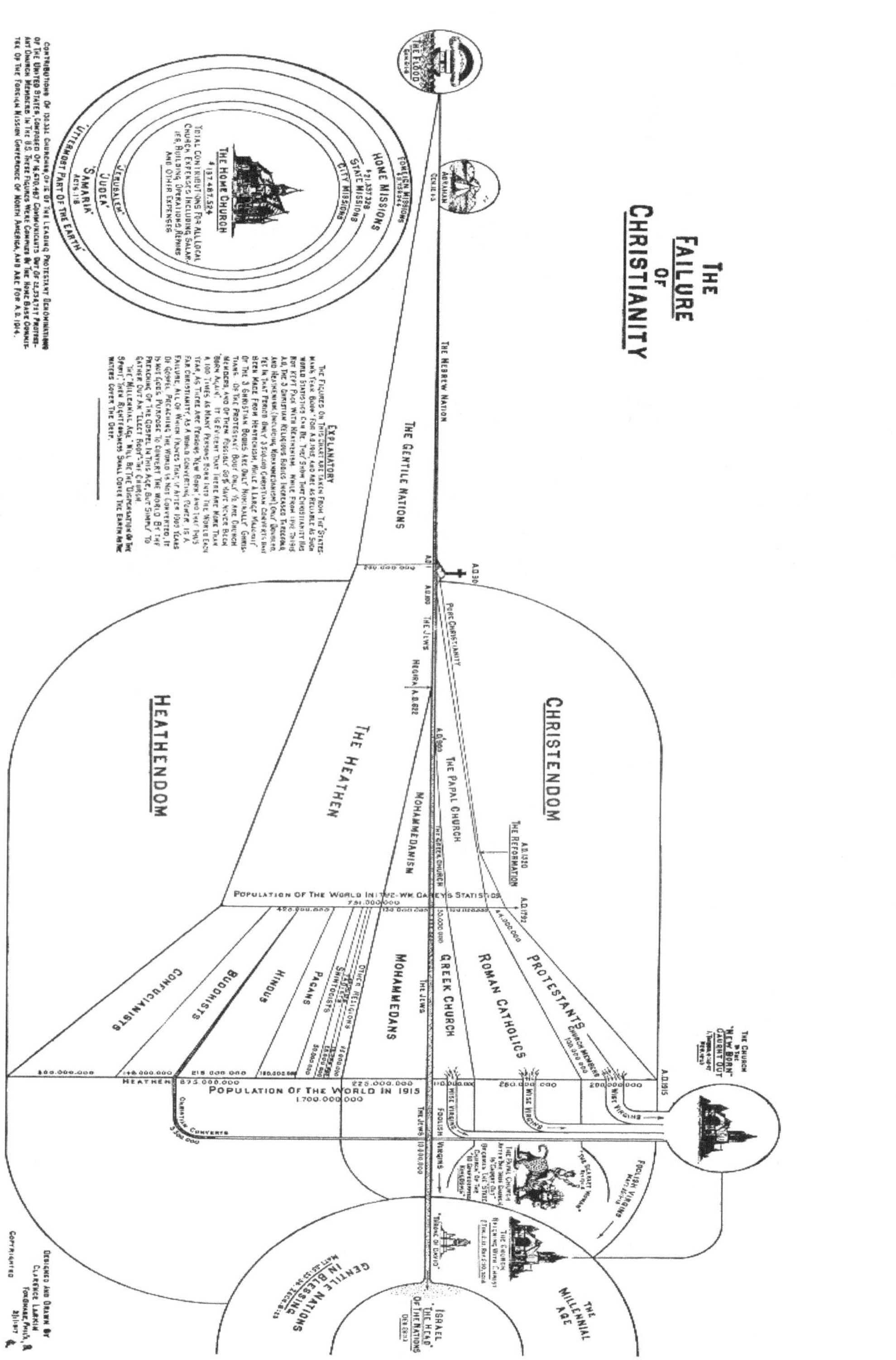
THE FAILURE OF CHRISTIANITY
CHRISTENDOM
HEATHENDOM
THE HEATHEN
THE PAPAL CHURCH
MOHAMMEDANISM
THE GENTILE NATIONS
THE HEBREW NATION
PROTESTANTS
ROMAN CATHOLICS
GREEK CHURCH
MOHAMMEDANS
PAGANS
HINDUS
BUDDHISTS
CONFUCIANISTS
POPULATION OF THE WORLD IN 1915
1.700.000.000
THE HOME CHURCH
HOME MISSIONS
THE MILLENNIAL AGE
GENTILE NATIONS IN BLESSING
EXPLANATORY

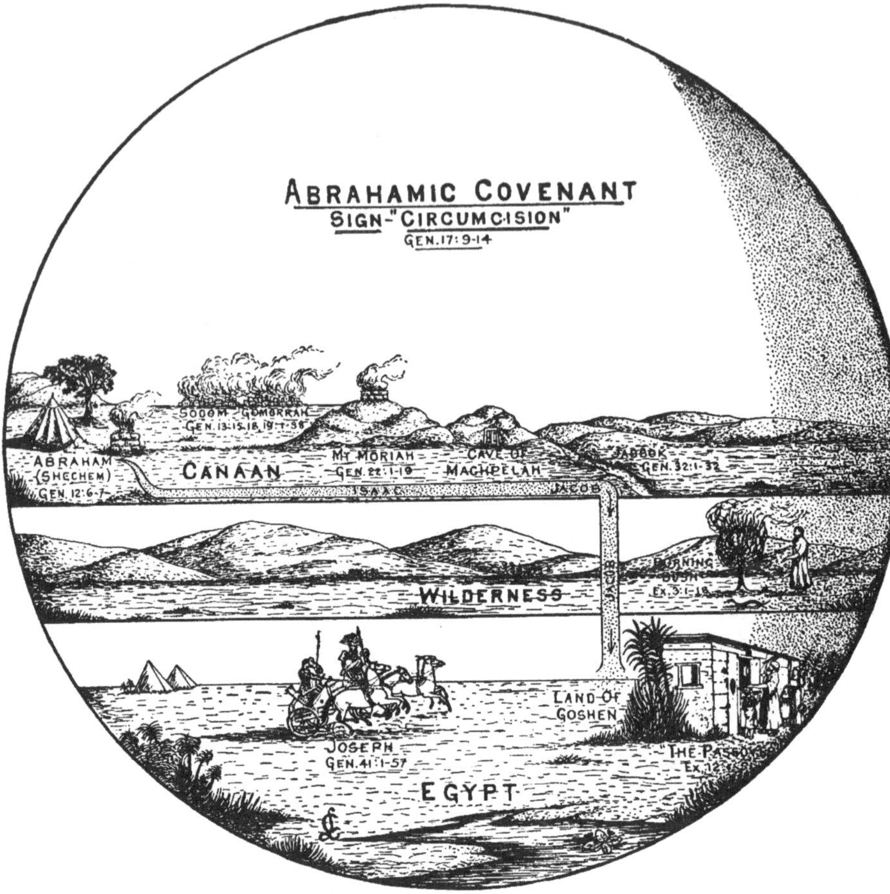

2. PATRIARCHAL DISPENSATION
(FAMILY)

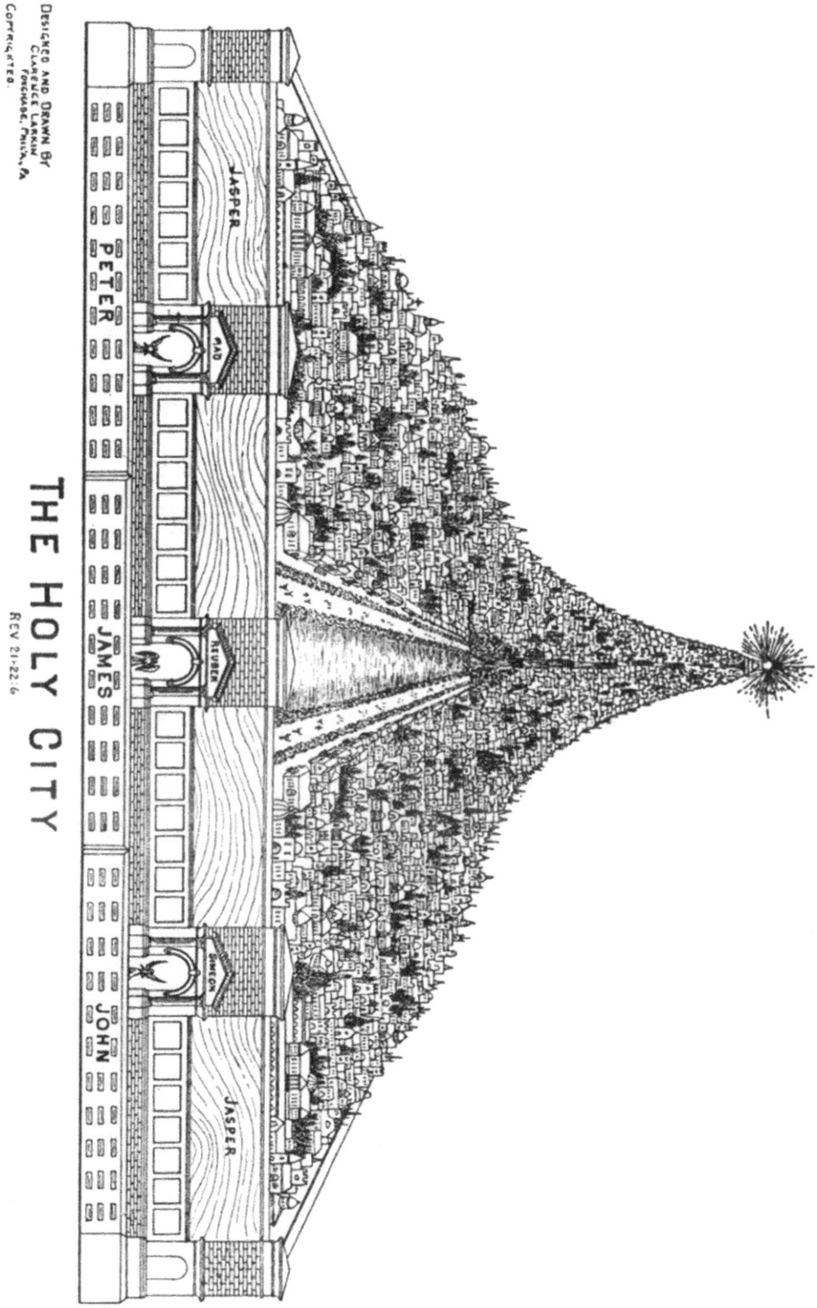
THE HOLY CITY
REV 21-22:6
PETER
JAMES
JOHN
JASPER
JASPER
GAD
REUBEN
SIMEON
DESIGNED AND DRAWN BY
CLARENCE LARKIN
FOXCHASE, PHILA, PA
COPYRIGHTED.

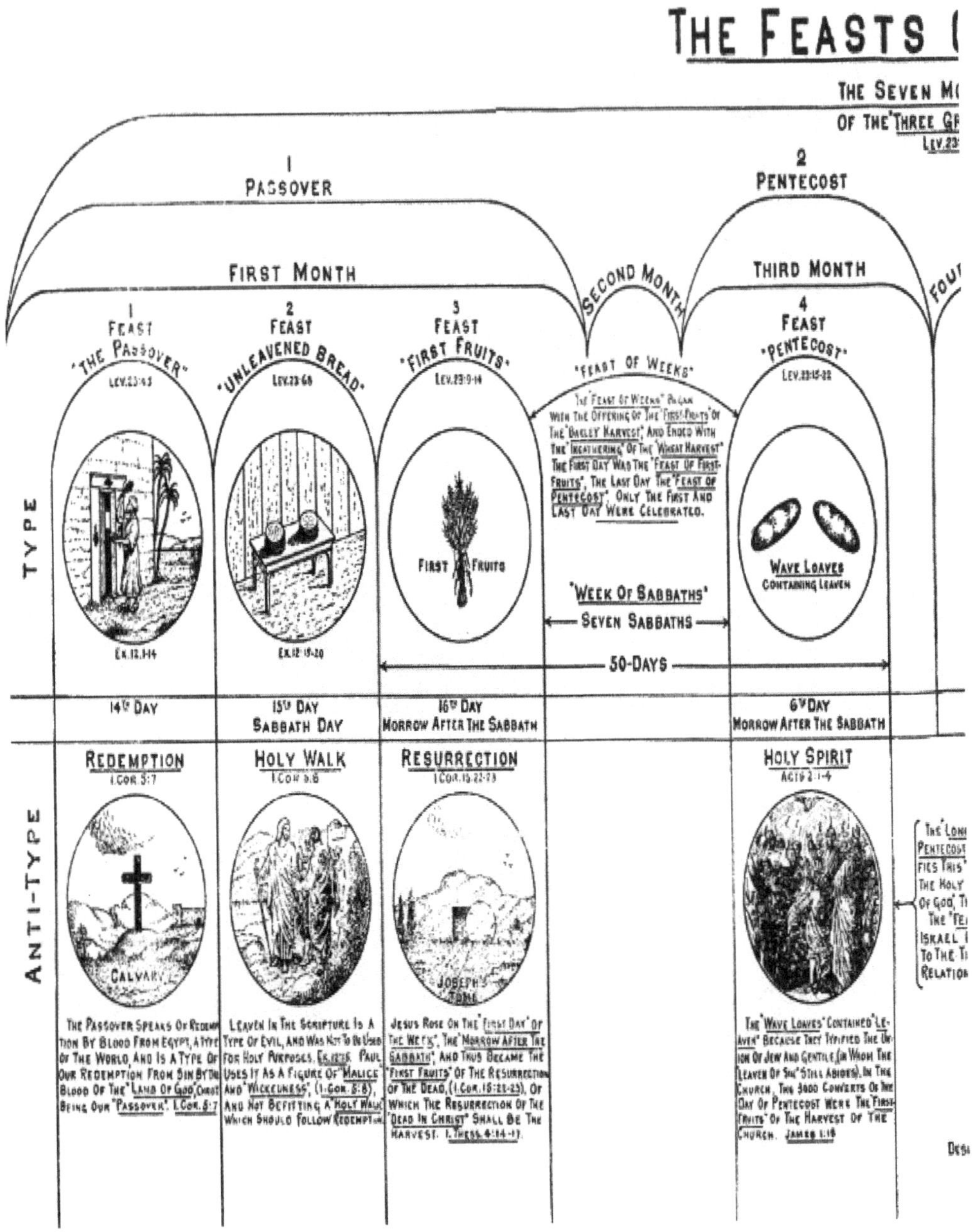
THE FEASTS (
THE SEVEN M(
OF THE "THREE GR
LEV.23
1
PASSOVER
2
PENTECOST
FIRST MONTH
SECOND MONTH
THIRD MONTH
1
FEAST
"THE PASSOVER"
LEV.23:4-5
2
FEAST
"UNLEAVENED BREAD"
LEV.23:6-8
3
FEAST
"FIRST FRUITS"
LEV.23:9-14
"FEAST OF WEEKS"
THE "FEAST OF WEEKS" BEGAN WITH THE OFFERING OF THE "FIRST-FRUITS" OF THE "BARLEY HARVEST", AND ENDED WITH THE "INGATHERING" OF THE "WHEAT HARVEST". THE FIRST DAY WAS THE "FEAST OF FIRST-FRUITS", THE LAST DAY THE "FEAST OF PENTECOST". ONLY THE FIRST AND LAST DAY WERE CELEBRATED.
4
FEAST
"PENTECOST"
LEV.23:15-22
TYPE
FIRST FRUITS
WAVE LOAVES
CONTAINING LEAVEN
"WEEK OF SABBATHS"
SEVEN SABBATHS
50-DAYS
EX.12:1-14
EX.12:15-20
14TH DAY
15TH DAY
SABBATH DAY
16TH DAY
MORROW AFTER THE SABBATH
6TH DAY
MORROW AFTER THE SABBATH
ANTI-TYPE
REDEMPTION
I.COR.5:7
HOLY WALK
I.COR.5:8
RESURRECTION
I.COR.15:22-23
HOLY SPIRIT
ACTS 2:1-4
CALVARY
JOSEPH'S TOMB
THE PASSOVER SPEAKS OF REDEMPTION BY BLOOD FROM EGYPT, A TYPE OF THE WORLD, AND IS A TYPE OF OUR REDEMPTION FROM SIN BY THE BLOOD OF THE "LAMB OF GOD", CHRIST BEING OUR "PASSOVER". I.COR.5:7
LEAVEN IN THE SCRIPTURE IS A TYPE OF EVIL, AND WAS NOT TO BE USED FOR HOLY PURPOSES. EX.12:15. PAUL USES IT AS A FIGURE OF "MALICE" AND "WICKEDNESS", (I.COR.5:8), AND NOT BEFITTING A "HOLY WALK" WHICH SHOULD FOLLOW REDEMPTION.
JESUS ROSE ON THE "FIRST DAY" OF THE WEEK", THE "MORROW AFTER THE SABBATH", AND THUS BECAME THE "FIRST FRUITS" OF THE RESURRECTION OF THE DEAD, (I.COR.15:22-23), OF WHICH THE RESURRECTION OF THE "DEAD IN CHRIST" SHALL BE THE HARVEST. I.THESS.4:14-17.
THE "WAVE LOAVES" CONTAINED "LEAVEN" BECAUSE THEY TYPIFIED THE UNION OF JEW AND GENTILE (IN WHOM THE "LEAVEN OF SIN" STILL ABIDES), IN THE CHURCH. THE 3000 CONVERTS OF THE DAY OF PENTECOST WERE THE "FIRST-FRUITS" OF THE HARVEST OF THE CHURCH. JAMES 1:18

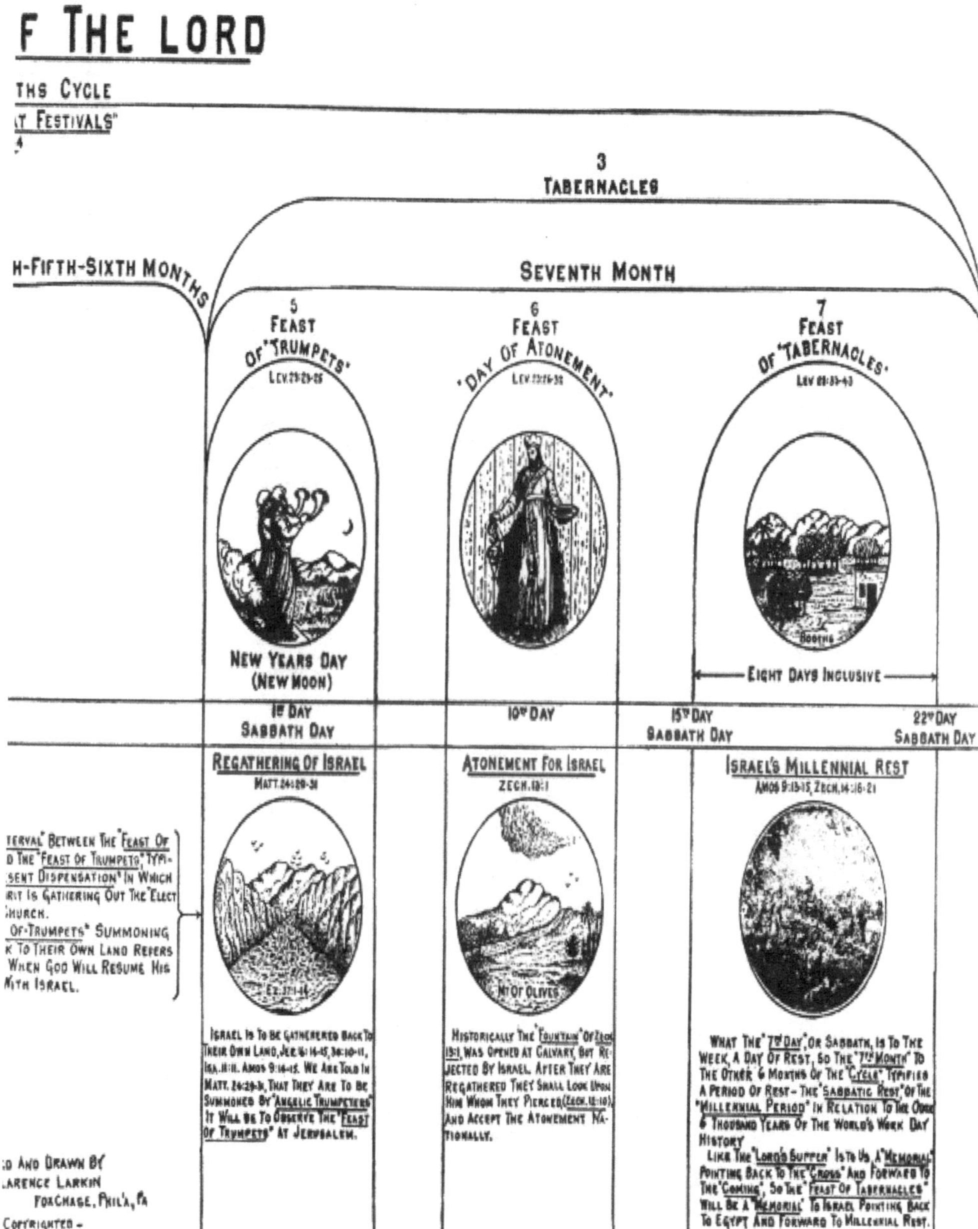
F THE LORD
THS CYCLE
T FESTIVALS"
3
TABERNACLES
H-FIFTH-SIXTH MONTHS
SEVENTH MONTH
5
FEAST
OF "TRUMPETS"
6
FEAST
"DAY OF ATONEMENT"
7
FEAST
OF "TABERNACLES"
BOOTHS
NEW YEARS DAY
(NEW MOON)
EIGHT DAYS INCLUSIVE
1ST DAY
SABBATH DAY
10TH DAY
15TH DAY
SABBATH DAY
22ND DAY
SABBATH DAY
REGATHERING OF ISRAEL
ATONEMENT FOR ISRAEL
ZECH.13:1
ISRAEL'S MILLENNIAL REST
TERVAL" BETWEEN THE "FEAST OF
D THE "FEAST OF TRUMPETS," TYPI-
SENT DISPENSATION" IN WHICH
RIT IS GATHERING OUT THE "ELECT
CHURCH.
OF-TRUMPETS" SUMMONING
K TO THEIR OWN LAND REFERS
WHEN GOD WILL RESUME HIS
WITH ISRAEL.
MT OF OLIVES
ISRAEL IS TO BE GATHERED BACK TO THEIR OWN LAND, JER.16:14-15, 30:10-11, ISA.11:11. AMOS 9:14-15. WE ARE TOLD IN MATT. 24:29-31, THAT THEY ARE TO BE SUMMONED BY "ANGELIC TRUMPETERS" IT WILL BE TO OBSERVE THE "FEAST OF TRUMPETS" AT JERUSALEM.
HISTORICALLY THE "FOUNTAIN" OF ZECH 13:1, WAS OPENED AT CALVARY, BUT REJECTED BY ISRAEL. AFTER THEY ARE REGATHERED THEY SHALL LOOK UPON HIM WHOM THEY PIERCED (ZECH. 12:10), AND ACCEPT THE ATONEMENT NATIONALLY.
WHAT THE "7TH DAY", OR SABBATH, IS TO THE WEEK, A DAY OF REST, SO THE "7TH MONTH" TO THE OTHER 6 MONTHS OF THE "CYCLE" TYPIFIES A PERIOD OF REST - THE "SABBATIC REST" OF THE "MILLENNIAL PERIOD" IN RELATION TO THE OTHER 6 THOUSAND YEARS OF THE WORLD'S WEEK DAY HISTORY
LIKE THE "LORD'S SUPPER" IS TO US A "MEMORIAL" POINTING BACK TO THE "CROSS" AND FORWARD TO THE "COMING", SO THE "FEAST OF TABERNACLES" WILL BE A "MEMORIAL" TO ISRAEL POINTING BACK TO EGYPT AND FORWARD TO MILLENNIAL REST.
D AND DRAWN BY
LARENCE LARKIN
FOXCHASE, PHIL'A, PA
COPYRIGHTED -

DANIEL AND REVELATION COMPARED

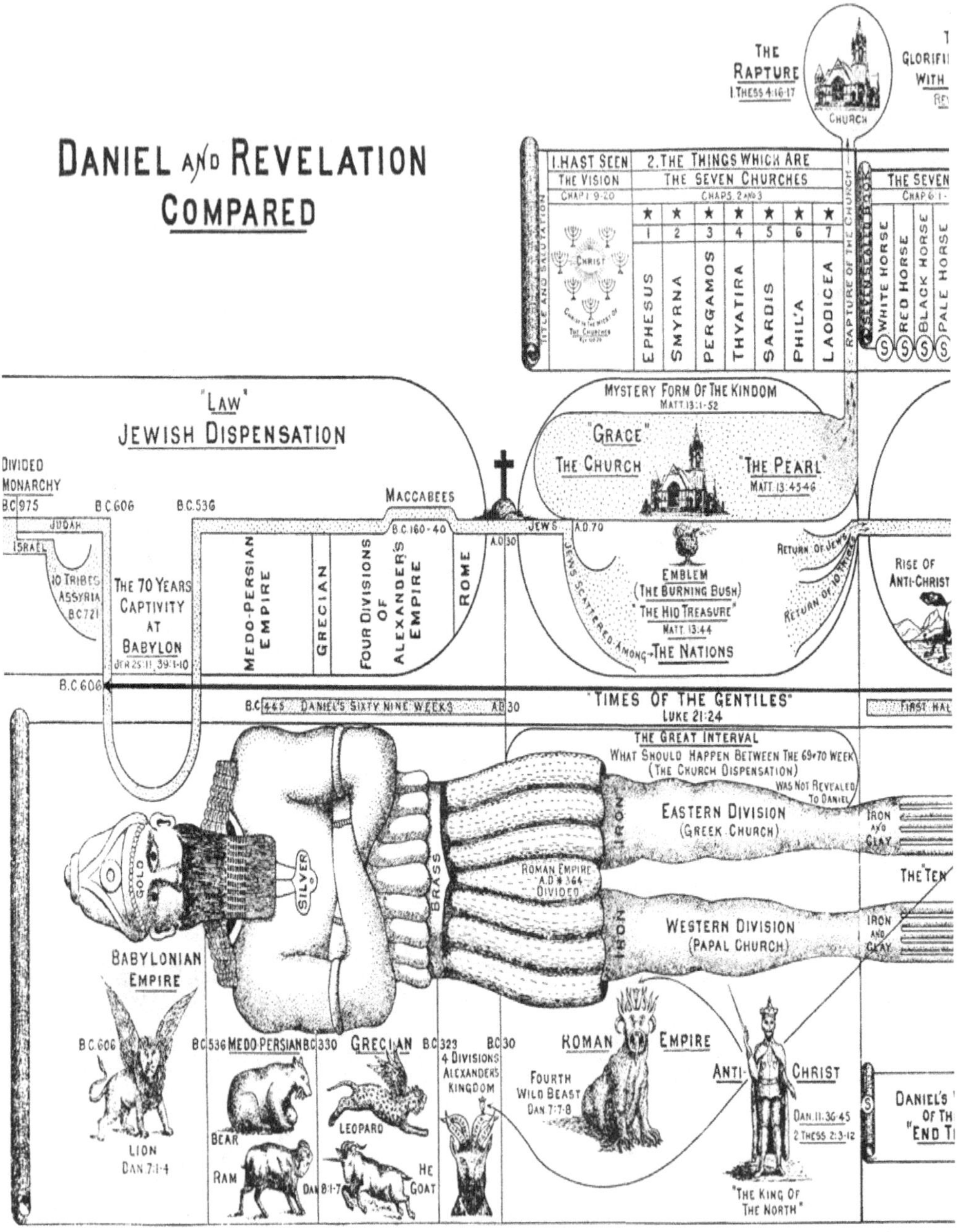

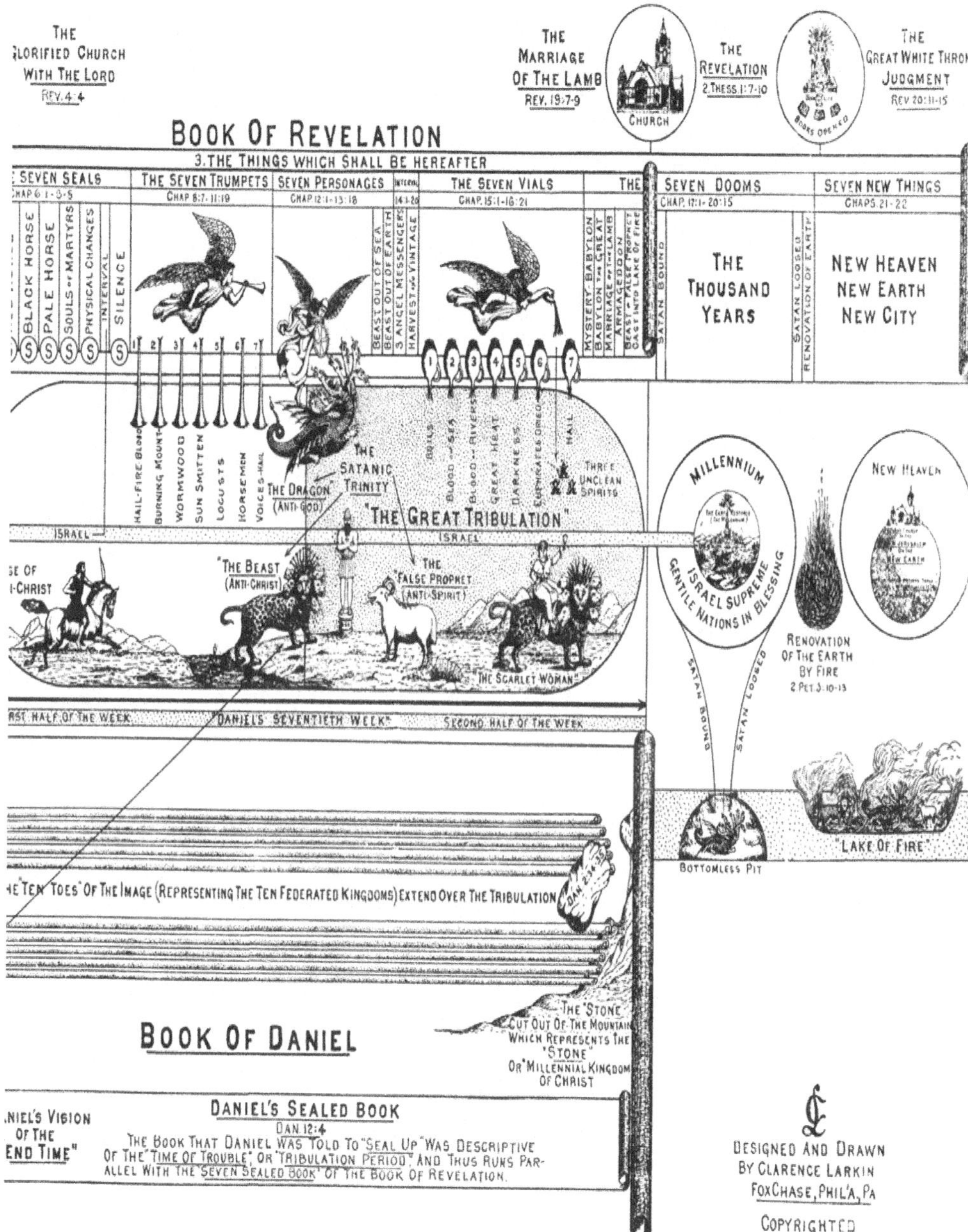

The Glorified Church With The Lord
Rev. 4:4
The Marriage Of The Lamb
Rev. 19:7-9
Church
The Revelation
2 Thess. 1:7-10
The Great White Throne Judgment
Rev. 20:11-15
Books Opened
Book Of Revelation
3. The Things Which Shall Be Hereafter
Seven Seals
Chap. 6:1-8:5
The Seven Trumpets
Chap. 8:7-11:19
Seven Personages
Chap. 12:1-13:18
The Seven Vials
Chap. 15:1-16:21
Seven Dooms
Chap. 17:1-20:15
Seven New Things
Chaps. 21-22
Black Horse
Pale Horse
Souls of Martyrs
Physical Changes
Interval
Silence
Hail-Fire Blood
Burning Mount
Wormwood
Sun Smitten
Locusts
Horsemen
Voices-Hail
Beast Out Of Sea
Beast Out Of Earth
3 Angel Messengers
Harvest and Vintage
Boils
Blood on Sea
Blood on Rivers
Great Heat
Darkness
Euphrates Dried
Hail
Mystery Babylon
Babylon the Great
Marriage of the Lamb
Armageddon
Beast and False Prophet Cast Into Lake Of Fire
Satan Bound
The Thousand Years
Satan Loosed
Renovation Of Earth
New Heaven
New Earth
New City
The Satanic Trinity
The Dragon (Anti-God)
Three Unclean Spirits
"The Great Tribulation"
Israel
"The Beast" (Anti-Christ)
"The False Prophet" (Anti-Spirit)
"The Scarlet Woman"
Millennium
Israel Supreme
Gentile Nations In Blessing
Satan Bound
Satan Loosed
Renovation Of The Earth By Fire
2 Pet. 3:10-13
New Heaven
New Earth
First Half Of The Week
"Daniel's Seventieth Week"
Second Half Of The Week
Bottomless Pit
"Lake Of Fire"
The "Ten Toes" Of The Image (Representing The Ten Federated Kingdoms) Extend Over The Tribulation
Dan. 2:34-35
The "Stone" Cut Out Of The Mountain Which Represents The "Stone" Or Millennial Kingdom Of Christ
Book Of Daniel
Daniel's Vision Of The "End Time"
Daniel's Sealed Book
Dan. 12:4
The Book That Daniel Was Told To "Seal Up" Was Descriptive Of The "Time Of Trouble", Or "Tribulation Period", And Thus Runs Parallel With The "Seven Sealed Book" Of The Book Of Revelation.
Designed And Drawn By Clarence Larkin
FoxChase, Phil'a, Pa
Copyrighted

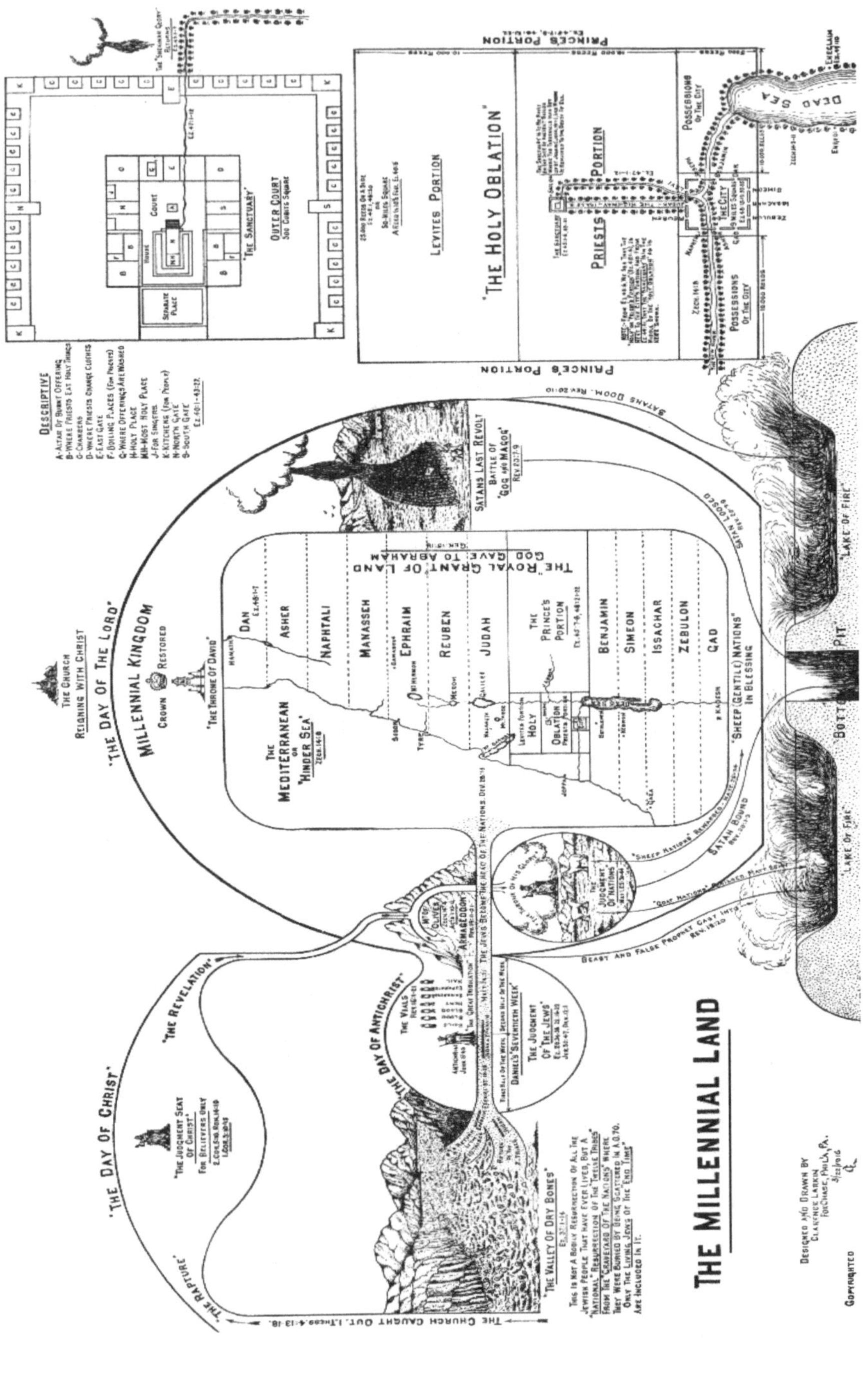
THE MILLENNIAL LAND
"THE DAY OF CHRIST"
"THE RAPTURE"
"THE REVELATION"
"THE DAY OF ANTICHRIST"
"THE DAY OF THE LORD"
THE CHURCH
REIGNING WITH CHRIST
MILLENNIAL KINGDOM
CROWN RESTORED
"THE THRONE OF DAVID"
"THE JUDGMENT SEAT OF CHRIST"
"THE VALLEY OF DRY BONES"
THE JUDGMENT OF "THE JEWS"
DANIEL'S SEVENTIETH WEEK
ARMAGEDDON
THE JUDGMENT OF "NATIONS"
THE MEDITERRANEAN OR "HINDER SEA"
THE "ROYAL GRANT" OF LAND
GOD GAVE TO ABRAHAM
DAN
ASHER
NAPHTALI
MANASSEH
EPHRAIM
REUBEN
JUDAH
THE PRINCE'S PORTION
BENJAMIN
SIMEON
ISSACHAR
ZEBULON
GAD
HOLY OBLATION
"SHEEP (GENTILE) NATIONS" IN BLESSING
SATAN BOUND
SATANS LAST REVOLT
BATTLE OF "GOG AND MAGOG"
SATAN LOOSED
SATANS DOOM
BEAST AND FALSE PROPHET CAST INTO
"LAKE OF FIRE"
"BOTTOMLESS PIT"
"LAKE OF FIRE"
DESCRIPTIVE
"THE SANCTUARY"
OUTER COURT
500 CUBITS SQUARE
"THE HOLY OBLATION"
LEVITES PORTION
PRIESTS PORTION
PRINCE'S PORTION
POSSESSIONS OF THE CITY
THE CITY
DEAD SEA
THE CHURCH CAUGHT OUT. I. THESS. 4:13-18.
DESIGNED AND DRAWN BY CLARENCE LARKIN
COPYRIGHTED

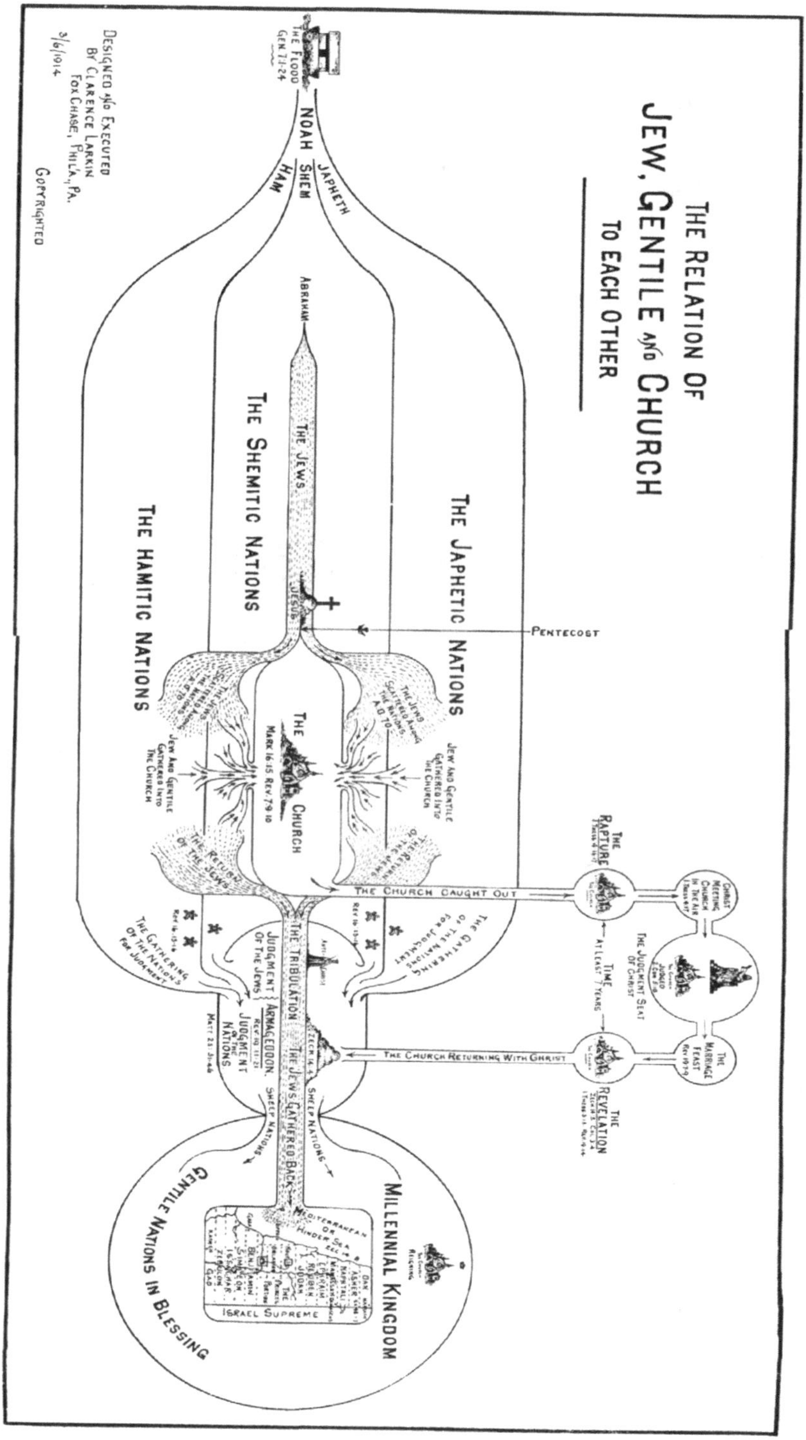
THE RELATION OF
JEW, GENTILE AND CHURCH
TO EACH OTHER
THE FLOOD
GEN. 7:1-24
NOAH
JAPHETH
SHEM
HAM
ABRAHAM
THE JEWS
JESUS
PENTECOST
THE JAPHETIC NATIONS
THE SHEMITIC NATIONS
THE HAMITIC NATIONS
THE JEWS SCATTERED AMONG THE NATIONS A.D. 70
JEW AND GENTILE GATHERED INTO THE CHURCH
THE CHURCH
MARK 16:15. REV. 7:9-10
THE RETURN OF THE JEWS
THE CHURCH CAUGHT OUT
THE RAPTURE
CHRIST MEETING CHURCH IN THE AIR
THE JUDGMENT SEAT OF CHRIST
TIME AT LEAST 7 YEARS
THE MARRIAGE FEAST
REV. 19:7-9
THE CHURCH RETURNING WITH CHRIST
THE REVELATION
THE GATHERING OF THE NATIONS FOR JUDGMENT
THE TRIBULATION
JUDGMENT OF THE JEWS
ARMAGEDDON
JUDGMENT OF THE NATIONS
MATT. 25:31-46
THE JEWS GATHERED BACK
SHEEP NATIONS
MILLENNIAL KINGDOM
GENTILE NATIONS IN BLESSING
ISRAEL SUPREME
DESIGNED AND EXECUTED
BY CLARENCE LARKIN
FOX CHASE, PHILA., PA.
3/6/1914
COPYRIGHTED

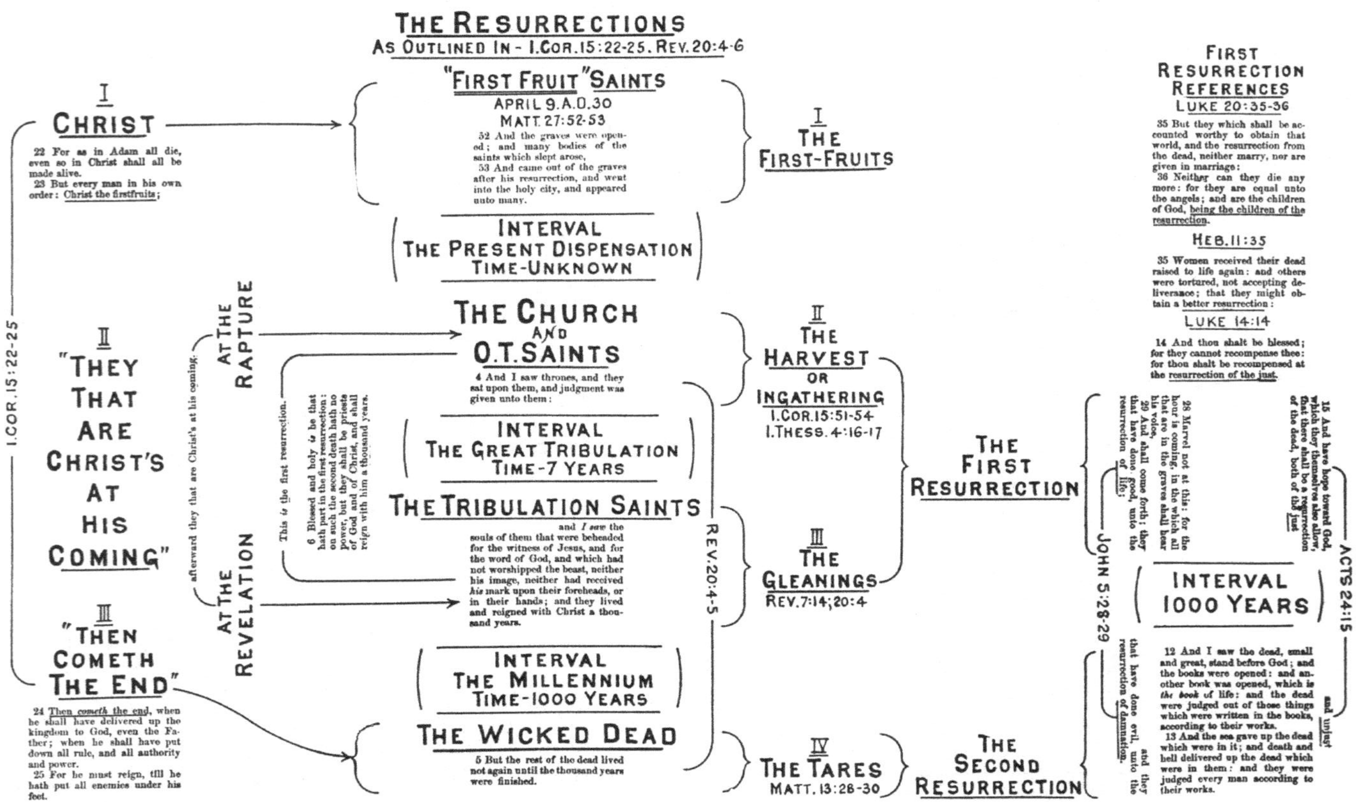
THE RESURRECTIONS
AS OUTLINED IN - I.COR.15:22-25. REV.20:4-6
I.COR.15:22-25
I
CHRIST
22 For as in Adam all die, even so in Christ shall all be made alive.
23 But every man in his own order: Christ the firstfruits;
II
"THEY THAT ARE CHRIST'S AT HIS COMING"
III
"THEN COMETH THE END"
24 Then cometh the end, when he shall have delivered up the kingdom to God, even the Father; when he shall have put down all rule, and all authority and power.
25 For he must reign, till he hath put all enemies under his feet.
afterward they that are Christ's at his coming.
AT THE RAPTURE
AT THE REVELATION
This is the first resurrection.
6 Blessed and holy is he that hath part in the first resurrection: on such the second death hath no power, but they shall be priests of God and of Christ, and shall reign with him a thousand years.
"FIRST FRUIT" SAINTS
APRIL 9. A.D.30
MATT.27:52-53
52 And the graves were opened; and many bodies of the saints which slept arose,
53 And came out of the graves after his resurrection, and went into the holy city, and appeared unto many.
INTERVAL
THE PRESENT DISPENSATION
TIME-UNKNOWN
THE CHURCH AND O.T. SAINTS
4 And I saw thrones, and they sat upon them, and judgment was given unto them:
INTERVAL
THE GREAT TRIBULATION
TIME-7 YEARS
THE TRIBULATION SAINTS
and I saw the souls of them that were beheaded for the witness of Jesus, and for the word of God, and which had not worshipped the beast, neither his image, neither had received his mark upon their foreheads, or in their hands; and they lived and reigned with Christ a thousand years.
INTERVAL
THE MILLENNIUM
TIME-1000 YEARS
THE WICKED DEAD
5 But the rest of the dead lived not again until the thousand years were finished.
REV.20:4-5
I
THE FIRST-FRUITS
II
THE HARVEST
OR
INGATHERING
I.COR.15:51-54
I.THESS.4:16-17
III
THE GLEANINGS
REV.7:14;20:4
IV
THE TARES
MATT.13:28-30
THE FIRST RESURRECTION
THE SECOND RESURRECTION
JOHN 5:28-29
28 Marvel not at this: for the hour is coming, in the which all that are in the graves shall hear his voice,
29 And shall come forth; they that have done good, unto the resurrection of life; and they that have done evil, unto the resurrection of damnation.
ACTS 24:15
15 And have hope toward God, which they themselves also allow, that there shall be a resurrection of the dead, both of the just and unjust.
INTERVAL
1000 YEARS
12 And I saw the dead, small and great, stand before God; and the books were opened: and another book was opened, which is the book of life: and the dead were judged out of those things which were written in the books, according to their works.
13 And the sea gave up the dead which were in it; and death and hell delivered up the dead which were in them: and they were judged every man according to their works.
FIRST RESURRECTION REFERENCES
LUKE 20:35-36
35 But they which shall be accounted worthy to obtain that world, and the resurrection from the dead, neither marry, nor are given in marriage:
36 Neither can they die any more: for they are equal unto the angels; and are the children of God, being the children of the resurrection.
HEB.11:35
35 Women received their dead raised to life again: and others were tortured, not accepting deliverance; that they might obtain a better resurrection:
LUKE 14:14
14 And thou shalt be blessed; for they cannot recompense thee: for thou shalt be recompensed at the resurrection of the just.

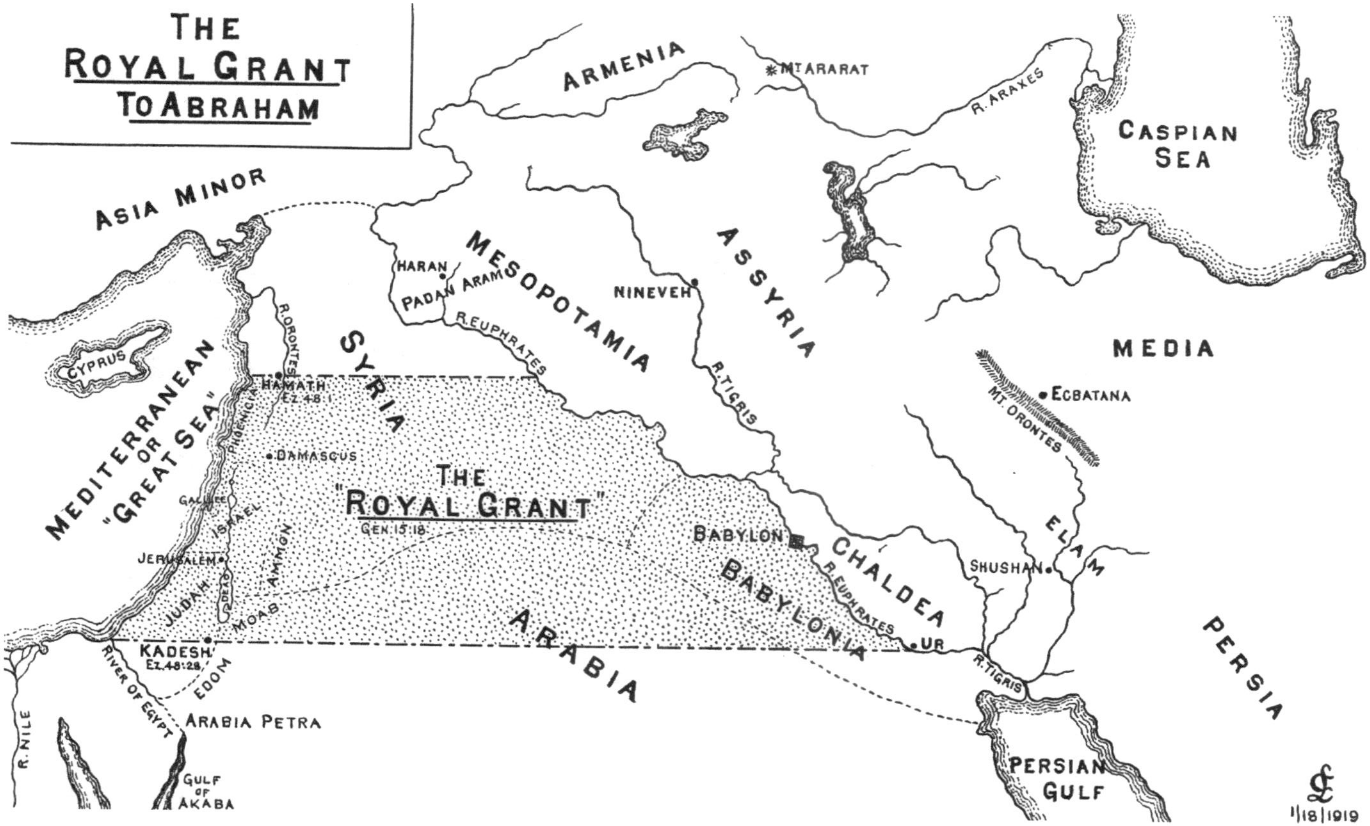
THE
ROYAL GRANT
TO ABRAHAM
ASIA MINOR
ARMENIA
MT. ARARAT
R. ARAXES
CASPIAN SEA
MESOPOTAMIA
HARAN
PADAN ARAM
NINEVEH
ASSYRIA
R. ORONTES
SYRIA
R. EUPHRATES
R. TIGRIS
MEDIA
ECBATANA
MT. ORONTES
CYPRUS
MEDITERRANEAN OR "GREAT SEA"
HAMATH
EZ. 48:1
PHOENICIA
DAMASCUS
THE "ROYAL GRANT"
GEN. 15:18
GALILEE
ISRAEL
JERUSALEM
JUDAH
DEAD
AMMON
MOAB
KADESH
EZ. 48:28
EDOM
RIVER OF EGYPT
R. NILE
ARABIA PETRA
GULF OF AKABA
ARABIA
BABYLON
BABYLONIA
CHALDEA
R. EUPHRATES
UR
R. TIGRIS
SHUSHAN
ELAM
PERSIA
PERSIAN GULF
1/18/1919

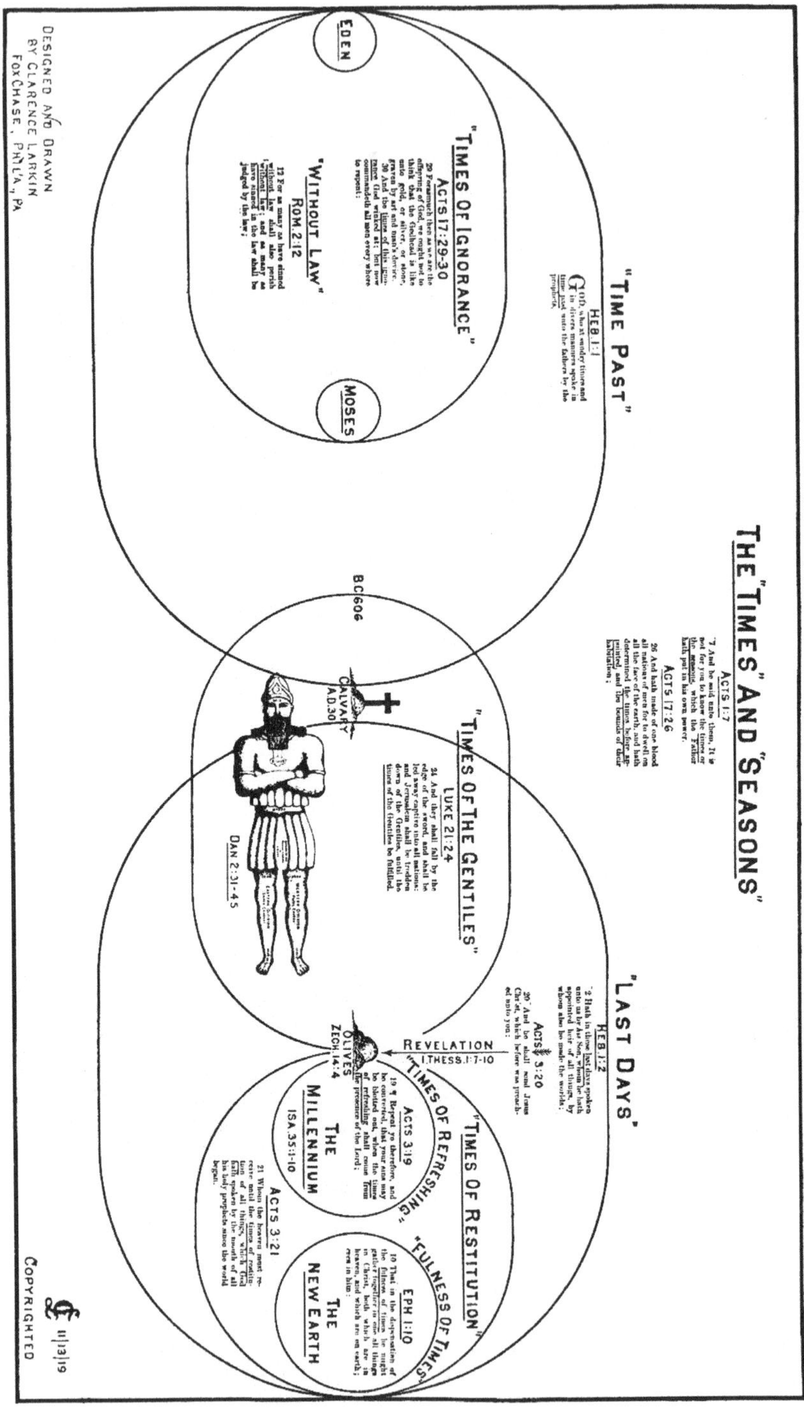

THE "TIMES" AND "SEASONS"
ACTS 1:7
ACTS 17:26
"TIME PAST"
HEB. 1:1
"LAST DAYS"
HEB. 1:2
ACTS 3:20
"TIMES OF IGNORANCE"
ACTS 17:29-30
"WITHOUT LAW"
ROM. 2:12
EDEN
MOSES
BC606
CALVARY
A.D.30
"TIMES OF THE GENTILES"
LUKE 21:24
DAN 2:31-45
REVELATION
I. THESS. 1:7-10
OLIVES
ZECH. 14:4
"TIMES OF REFRESHING"
ACTS 3:19
THE MILLENNIUM
ISA. 35:1-10
"TIMES OF RESTITUTION"
ACTS 3:21
"FULNESS OF TIMES"
EPH. 1:10
THE NEW EARTH
DESIGNED AND DRAWN
BY CLARENCE LARKIN
FOX CHASE, PHIL'A., PA
COPYRIGHTED

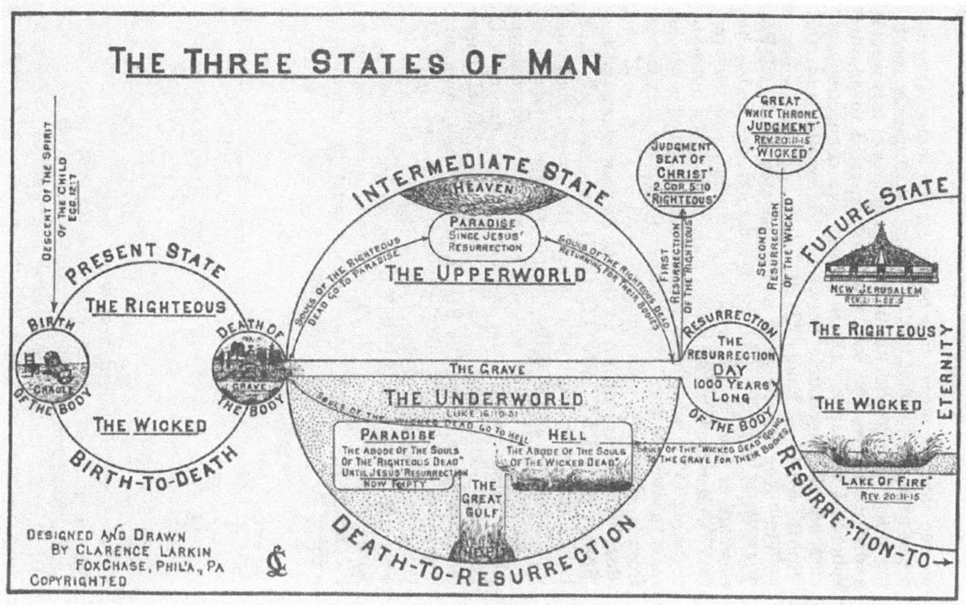
THE THREE STATES OF MAN
DESCENT OF THE SPIRIT
OF THE CHILD
ECC. 12:7
PRESENT STATE
BIRTH
CRADLE
OF THE BODY
THE RIGHTEOUS
THE WICKED
BIRTH-TO-DEATH
DEATH OF
GRAVE
THE BODY
INTERMEDIATE STATE
HEAVEN
PARADISE
SINCE JESUS' RESURRECTION
SOULS OF THE RIGHTEOUS DEAD GO TO PARADISE
SOULS OF THE RIGHTEOUS DEAD RETURNING FOR THEIR BODIES
THE UPPERWORLD
THE GRAVE
THE UNDERWORLD
LUKE 16:19-31
SOULS OF THE WICKED DEAD GO TO HELL
PARADISE
THE ABODE OF THE SOULS OF THE "RIGHTEOUS DEAD" UNTIL JESUS' RESURRECTION
NOW EMPTY
HELL
THE ABODE OF THE SOULS OF THE WICKED DEAD
THE GREAT GULF
DEATH-TO-RESURRECTION
JUDGMENT SEAT OF CHRIST
2. COR. 5:10
"RIGHTEOUS"
FIRST RESURRECTION OF THE RIGHTEOUS
GREAT WHITE THRONE JUDGMENT
REV. 20:11-15
"WICKED"
SECOND RESURRECTION OF THE "WICKED"
RESURRECTION
THE RESURRECTION DAY
1000 YEARS LONG
OF THE BODY
SOULS OF THE "WICKED DEAD" GOING TO THE GRAVE FOR THEIR BODIES
FUTURE STATE
NEW JERUSALEM
REV. 21:1-22:5
THE RIGHTEOUS
THE WICKED
"LAKE OF FIRE"
REV. 20:11-15
ETERNITY
RESURRECTION-TO→
DESIGNED AND DRAWN
BY CLARENCE LARKIN
FOXCHASE, PHIL'A., PA
COPYRIGHTED

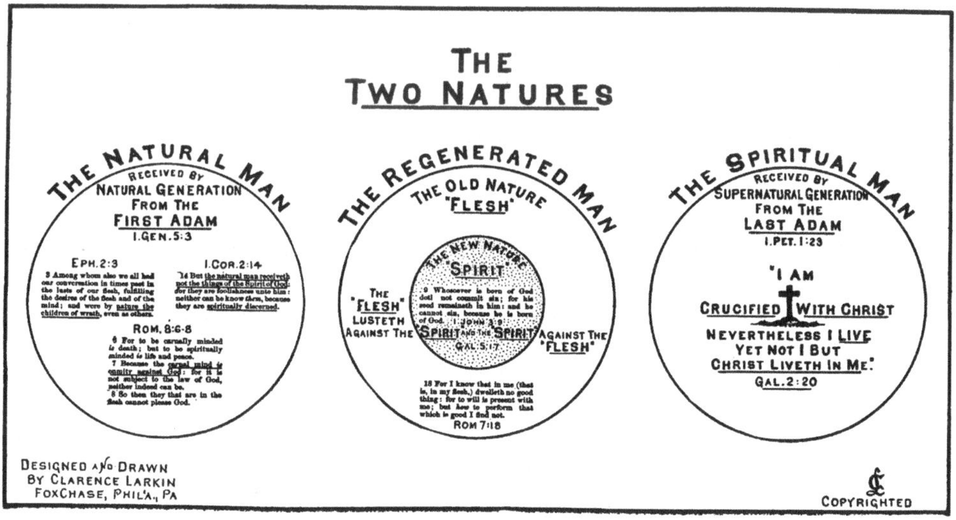
THE TWO NATURES
THE NATURAL MAN
RECEIVED BY
NATURAL GENERATION
FROM THE
FIRST ADAM
I. GEN. 5:3
EPH. 2:3
3 Among whom also we all had our conversation in times past in the lusts of our flesh, fulfilling the desires of the flesh and of the mind; and were by nature the children of wrath, even as others.
I. COR. 2:14
14 But the natural man receiveth not the things of the Spirit of God: for they are foolishness unto him: neither can he know them, because they are spiritually discerned.
ROM. 8:6-8
6 For to be carnally minded is death; but to be spiritually minded is life and peace.
7 Because the carnal mind is enmity against God: for it is not subject to the law of God, neither indeed can be.
8 So then they that are in the flesh cannot please God.
THE REGENERATED MAN
THE OLD NATURE
"FLESH"
THE NEW NATURE
"SPIRIT"
9 Whosoever is born of God doth not commit sin; for his seed remaineth in him: and he cannot sin, because he is born of God. I. JOHN 3:9
THE "FLESH" LUSTETH AGAINST THE "SPIRIT" AND THE "SPIRIT" AGAINST THE "FLESH"
GAL. 5:17
18 For I know that in me (that is, in my flesh,) dwelleth no good thing: for to will is present with me; but how to perform that which is good I find not.
ROM 7:18
THE SPIRITUAL MAN
RECEIVED BY
SUPERNATURAL GENERATION
FROM THE
LAST ADAM
I. PET. 1:23
"I AM
CRUCIFIED WITH CHRIST
NEVERTHELESS I LIVE
YET NOT I BUT
CHRIST LIVETH IN ME."
GAL. 2:20
DESIGNED AND DRAWN
BY CLARENCE LARKIN
FOXCHASE, PHIL'A., PA
COPYRIGHTED

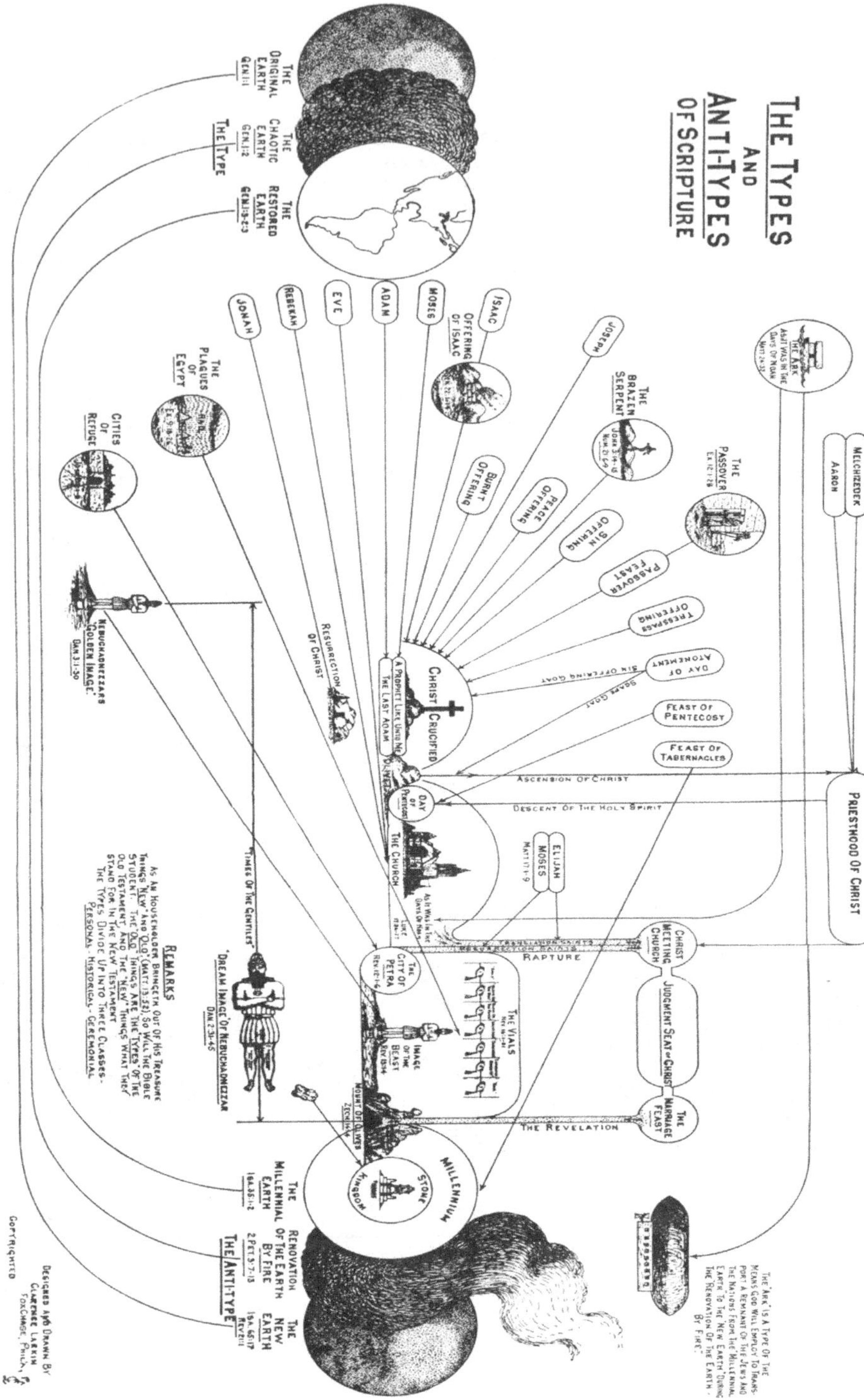
THE TYPES AND ANTI-TYPES OF SCRIPTURE
THE ORIGINAL EARTH
THE CHAOTIC EARTH
THE RESTORED EARTH
THE TYPE
MOSES
ADAM
EVE
REBEKAH
JONAH
ISAAC
JOSEPH
THE BRAZEN SERPENT
THE PASSOVER
BURNT OFFERING
PEACE OFFERING
SIN OFFERING
PASSOVER FEAST
TRESPASS OFFERING
DAY OF ATONEMENT
FEAST OF PENTECOST
FEAST OF TABERNACLES
MELCHIZEDEK
AARON
PRIESTHOOD OF CHRIST
CHRIST CRUCIFIED
THE CHURCH
ELIJAH
MOSES
RAPTURE
JUDGMENT SEAT OF CHRIST
THE REVELATION
MILLENNIUM
THE MILLENNIAL EARTH
THE RENOVATION OF THE EARTH BY FIRE
THE NEW EARTH
THE ANTI-TYPE
REMARKS
COPYRIGHTED

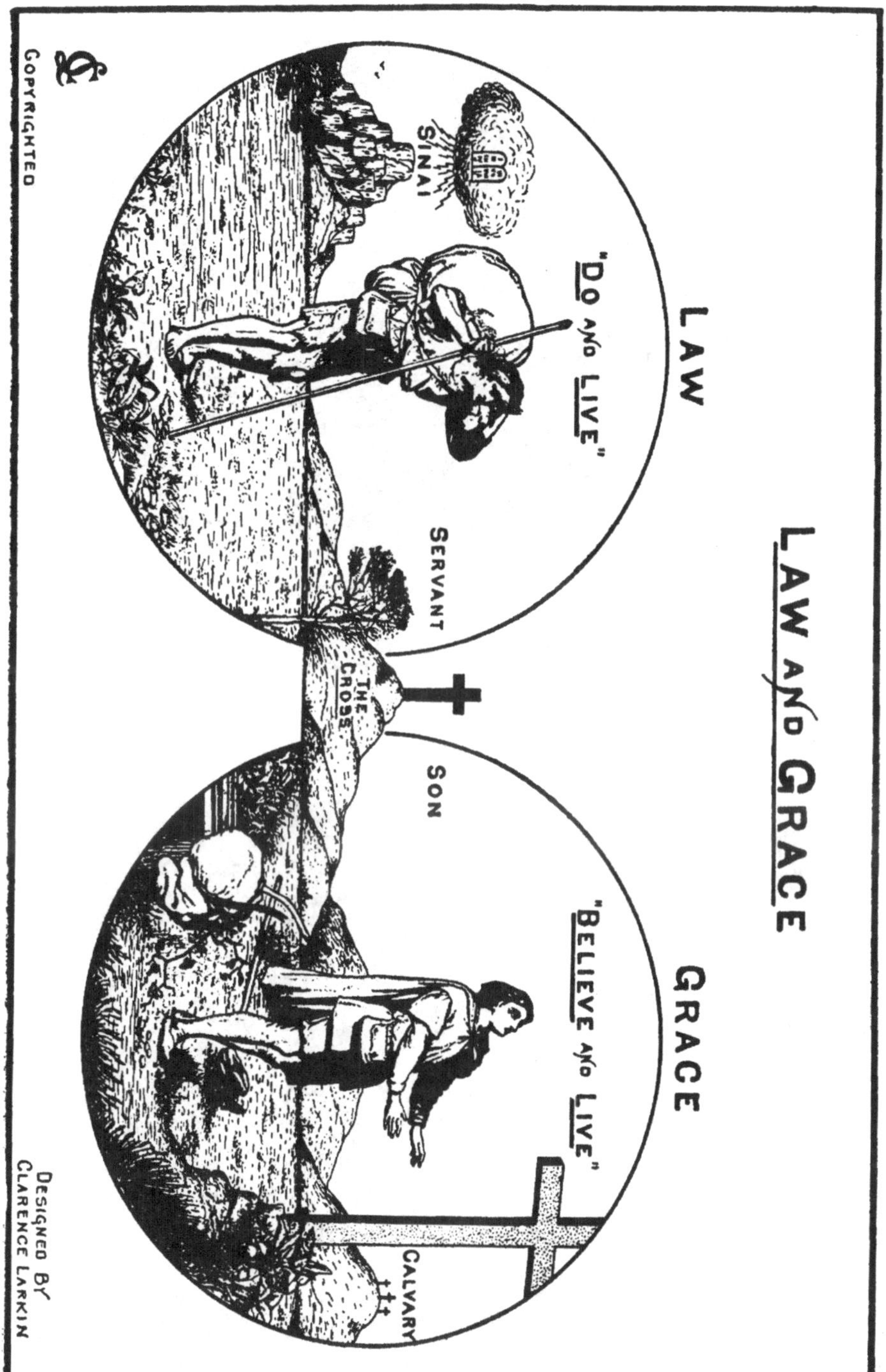
LAW AND GRACE
LAW
"DO AND LIVE"
SINAI
SERVANT
THE CROSS
SON
GRACE
"BELIEVE AND LIVE"
CALVARY
COPYRIGHTED
DESIGNED BY
CLARENCE LARKIN

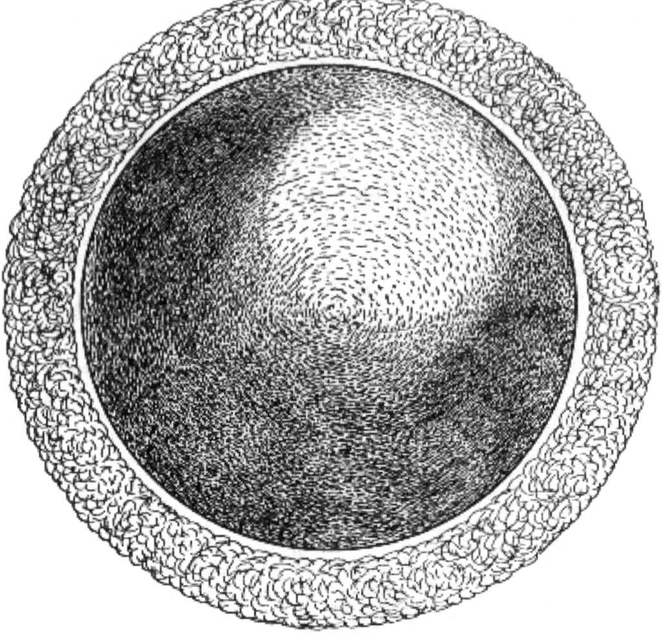

SECOND DAY
FIRMAMENT FORMED

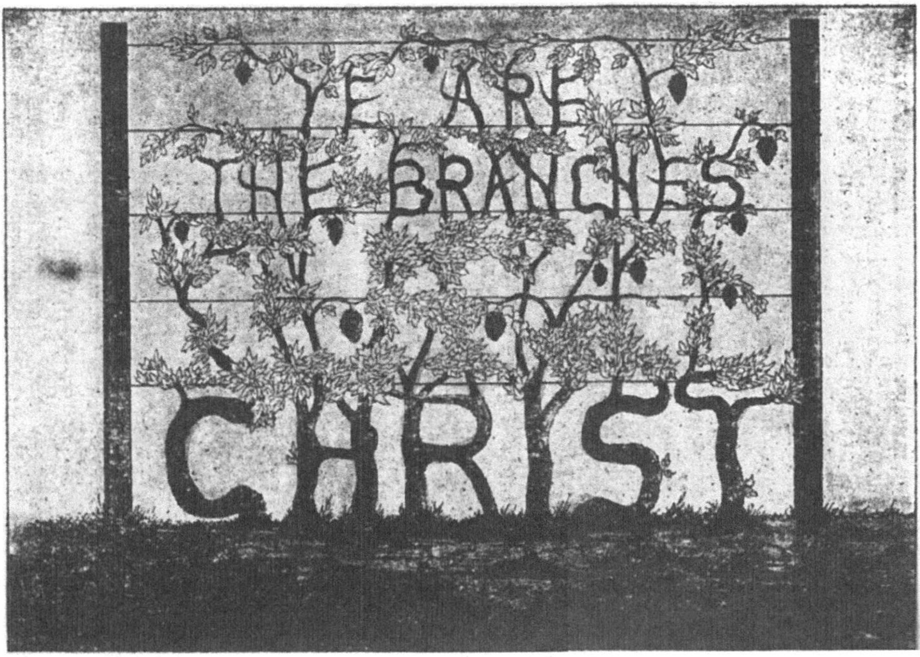

FIFTH DAY
CREATION OF FISH AND FOWL

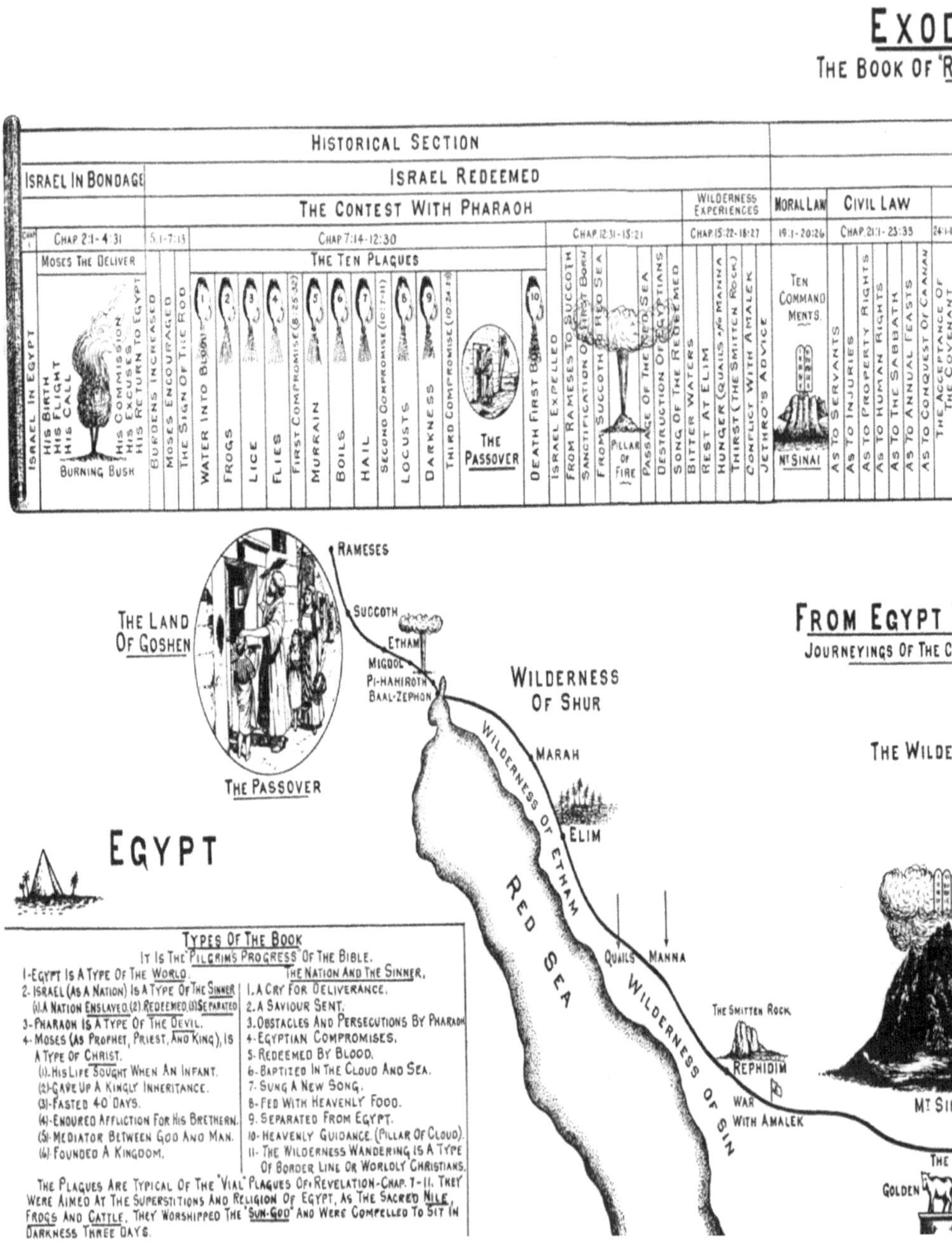
EXOD
THE BOOK OF 'R
HISTORICAL SECTION
ISRAEL IN BONDAGE
ISRAEL REDEEMED
THE CONTEST WITH PHARAOH
WILDERNESS EXPERIENCES
MORAL LAW
CIVIL LAW
CHAP 2:1-4:31
5:1-7:13
CHAP 7:14-12:30
CHAP 12:31-15:21
CHAP 15:22-18:27
19:1-20:26
CHAP 21:1-23:33
MOSES THE DELIVER
THE TEN PLAGUES
ISRAEL IN EGYPT
HIS BIRTH
HIS FLIGHT
HIS CALL
HIS COMMISSION
HIS EXCUSES
HIS RETURN TO EGYPT
BURNING BUSH
BURDENS INCREASED
MOSES ENCOURAGED
THE SIGN OF THE ROD
WATER INTO BLOOD
FROGS
LICE
FLIES
FIRST COMPROMISE (8:25-32)
MURRAIN
BOILS
HAIL
SECOND COMPROMISE (10:7-11)
LOCUSTS
DARKNESS
THIRD COMPROMISE (10:24-29)
THE PASSOVER
DEATH FIRST BORN
ISRAEL EXPELLED
FROM RAMESES TO SUCCOTH
SANCTIFICATION OF FIRST BORN
FROM SUCCOTH TO RED SEA
PILLAR OF FIRE
PASSAGE OF THE RED SEA
DESTRUCTION OF EGYPTIANS
SONG OF THE REDEEMED
BITTER WATERS
REST AT ELIM
HUNGER (QUAILS AND MANNA)
THIRST (THE SMITTEN ROCK)
CONFLICT WITH AMALEK
JETHRO'S ADVICE
TEN COMMANDMENTS
MT SINAI
AS TO SERVANTS
AS TO INJURIES
AS TO PROPERTY RIGHTS
AS TO HUMAN RIGHTS
AS TO THE SABBATH
AS TO ANNUAL FEASTS
AS TO CONQUEST OF CANAAN
THE ACCEPTANCE OF THE COVENANT
RAMESES
SUCCOTH
ETHAM
MIGDOL
PI-HAHIROTH
BAAL-ZEPHON
THE LAND OF GOSHEN
THE PASSOVER
WILDERNESS OF SHUR
WILDERNESS OF ETHAM
MARAH
ELIM
EGYPT
RED SEA
QUAILS
MANNA
WILDERNESS OF SIN
THE SMITTEN ROCK
REPHIDIM
WAR WITH AMALEK
FROM EGYPT
JOURNEYINGS OF THE CH
THE WILDE
MT SIN
THE GOLDEN
TYPES OF THE BOOK
IT IS THE "PILGRIM'S PROGRESS" OF THE BIBLE.
1-EGYPT IS A TYPE OF THE WORLD.
2-ISRAEL (AS A NATION) IS A TYPE OF THE SINNER
(1) A NATION ENSLAVED. (2) REDEEMED. (3) SEPARATED
3-PHARAOH IS A TYPE OF THE DEVIL.
4-MOSES (AS PROPHET, PRIEST, AND KING), IS A TYPE OF CHRIST.
(1)-HIS LIFE SOUGHT WHEN AN INFANT.
(2)-GAVE UP A KINGLY INHERITANCE.
(3)-FASTED 40 DAYS.
(4)-ENDURED AFFLICTION FOR HIS BRETHERN.
(5)-MEDIATOR BETWEEN GOD AND MAN.
(6)-FOUNDED A KINGDOM.
THE NATION AND THE SINNER.
1. A CRY FOR DELIVERANCE.
2. A SAVIOUR SENT.
3. OBSTACLES AND PERSECUTIONS BY PHARAOH
4-EGYPTIAN COMPROMISES.
5-REDEEMED BY BLOOD.
6-BAPTIZED IN THE CLOUD AND SEA.
7-SUNG A NEW SONG.
8-FED WITH HEAVENLY FOOD.
9. SEPARATED FROM EGYPT.
10-HEAVENLY GUIDANCE. (PILLAR OF CLOUD).
11-THE WILDERNESS WANDERING IS A TYPE OF BORDER LINE OR WORLDLY CHRISTIANS.
THE PLAGUES ARE TYPICAL OF THE "VIAL" PLAGUES OF REVELATION-CHAP. 7-11. THEY WERE AIMED AT THE SUPERSTITIONS AND RELIGION OF EGYPT, AS THE SACRED NILE, FROGS AND CATTLE. THEY WORSHIPPED THE "SUN-GOD" AND WERE COMPELLED TO SIT IN DARKNESS THREE DAYS.

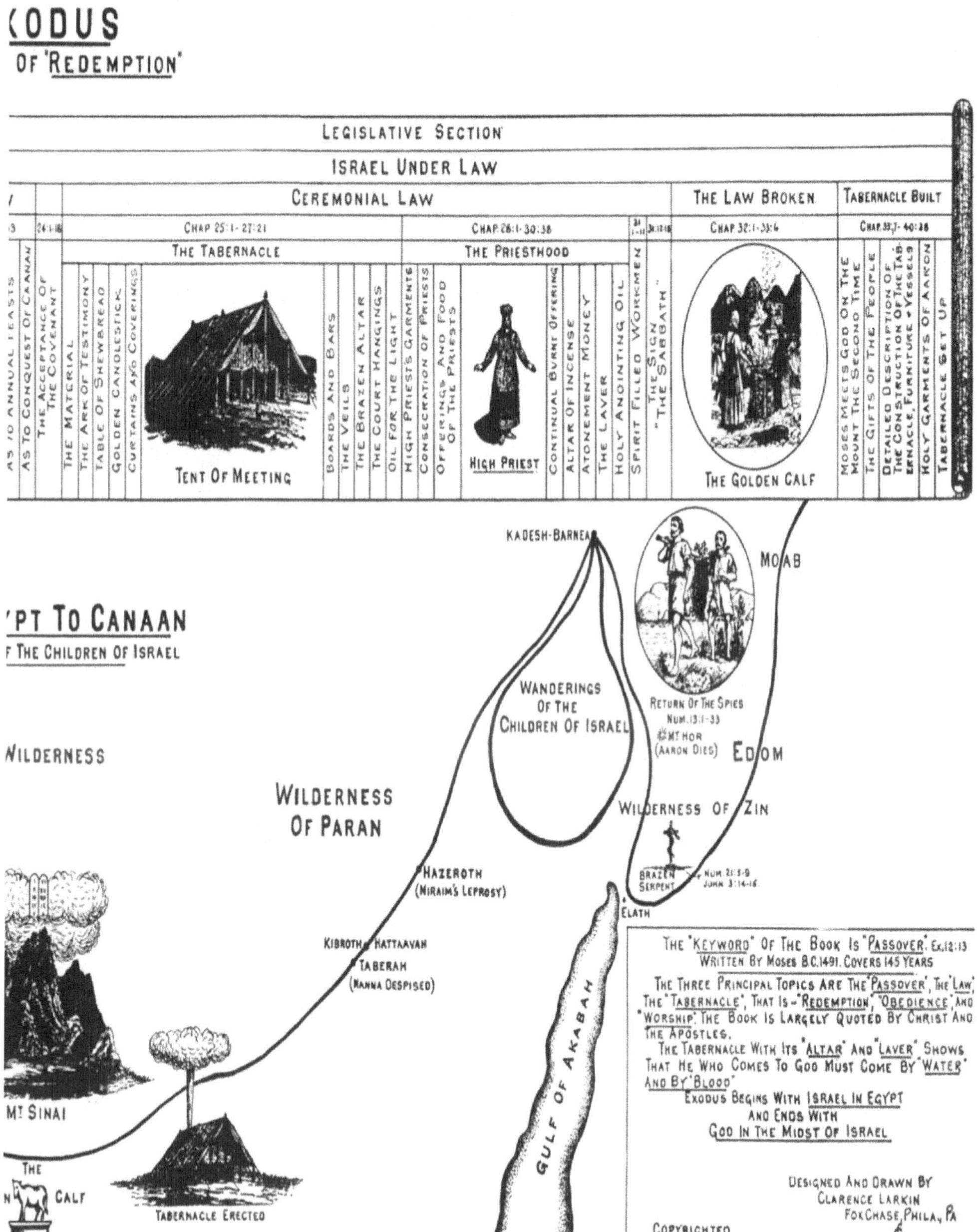

THE "KEYWORD" OF THE BOOK IS "PASSOVER". Ex.12:13
WRITTEN BY MOSES B.C.1491. COVERS 145 YEARS

THE THREE PRINCIPAL TOPICS ARE THE "PASSOVER", THE "LAW", THE "TABERNACLE", THAT IS - "REDEMPTION", "OBEDIENCE", AND "WORSHIP". THE BOOK IS LARGELY QUOTED BY CHRIST AND THE APOSTLES.

THE TABERNACLE WITH ITS "ALTAR" AND "LAVER" SHOWS THAT HE WHO COMES TO GOD MUST COME BY "WATER" AND BY "BLOOD".

EXODUS BEGINS WITH ISRAEL IN EGYPT
AND ENDS WITH
GOD IN THE MIDST OF ISRAEL

DESIGNED AND DRAWN BY
CLARENCE LARKIN
FOX CHASE, PHILA., PA

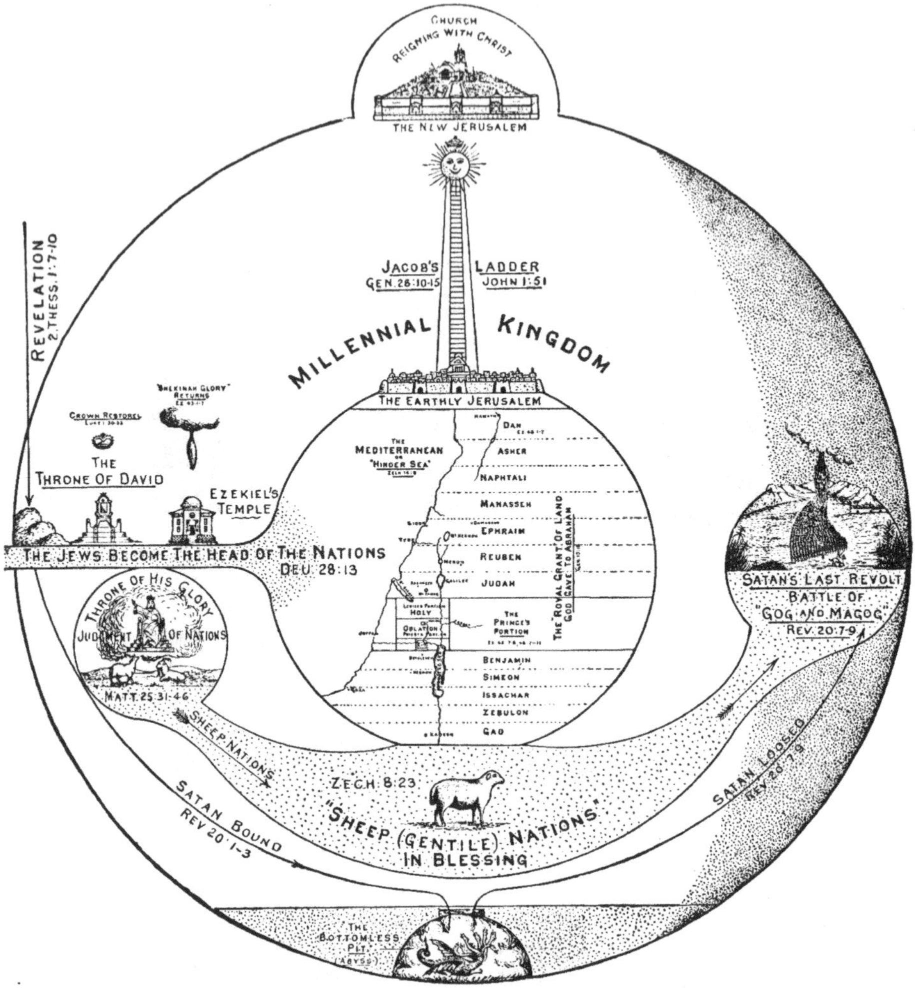

MESSIANIC DISPENSATION
(RIGHTEOUSNESS)

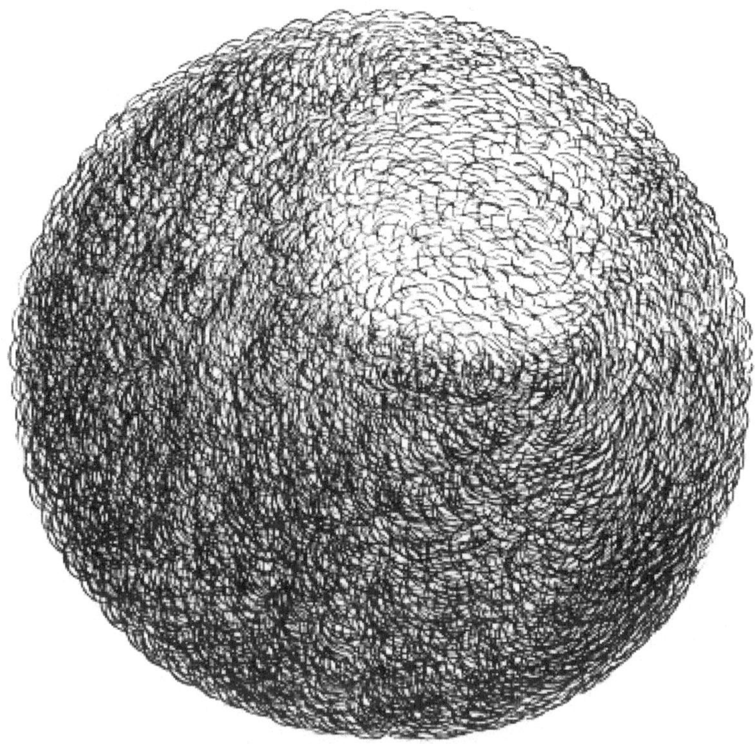

FIRST DAY
COSMIC LIGHT

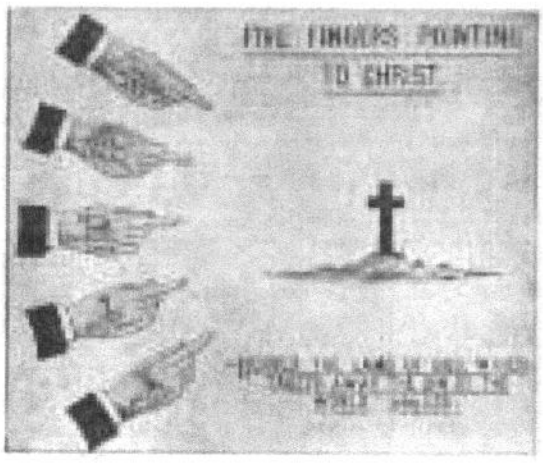

LEVI

THE BOOK O

THE WAY TO GOD THROUGH SACRIFICE																	
THE OFFERINGS										THE PRIESTHOOD			LAWS OF PURITY				
SWEET SAVOUR OFFERINGS			SIN OFFERINGS		LAW OF THE OFFERINGS								AS TO THE PEOPLE				
CHAP. 1:1-3:17			CHAP. 4:1-6:7		CHAP. 6:8-7:38					8:1-36	9:1-24	10:1-20	11:1-47	12:1-8	13:1-14:57	15:1-33	CHAP. 16
1 BURNT OFFERING	2 MEAL OFFERING	3 PEACE OFFERING	4 SIN OFFERING	5 TRESPASS OFFERING	BURNT OFFERING	MEAL OFFERING	SIN OFFERING	TRESPASS OFFERING	PEACE OFFERING	CONSECRATION OF AARON AND HIS SONS	WORK OF THE PRIEST	PUNISHMENT OF PRIESTS	AS TO FOOD	AS TO MOTHERHOOD	AS TO LEPROSY	AS TO UNCLEANNESS	THE DA ATONE
THESE OFFERINGS ARE DESCRIBED BELOW																	

THE LEVITICAL OFFERINGS

OFFERINGS	THE OFFERING	THE OFFERER'S WORK	THE PRIEST'S WORK	GOD'S PORTION	THE PRIEST'S PORTION	THE OFFERER'S PORTION	SYMBOLISM
BURNT OFFERING	A Bullock, or a Sheep, or a Goat, or Turtle Doves or Young Pigeons, according to the ability of the Offerer. If of the Herd or Flock, a year old and without blemish.	He led it to the Door of the Tabernacle, laid his hand on it, slew, skinned, cut in peices, washed the parts and gave to Priest. When a fowl he handed it to the Priest. Lev. 1:14-17	He caught the Blood, sprinkled it around the Altar and placed the parts in order on the Altar. Thus it was called a "Whole" Burnt Offering.	All that was burned	The Skin. Lev. 7:8	Nothing	Complete Consecr tion of the Offere to God. Rom. 12:1
MEAL OFFERING	Unbaked Flour ground fine, or baked Cakes, or green ears of Corn, parched or roasted. It was to be mixed with Oil, seasoned with Salt, sprinkled with Frankincense. Contain no Leaven or Honey	He simply brought the Offering to the Priest.	He threw a handful of the Offering, and all the Frankincense, on the Altar Fire.	The handful of the Offering and the Frankincense.	The remainder of the Offering. Lev. 6:14-18.	Nothing	The Consecration Offerer's Toil and P sessions to God.
PEACE OFFERING	A Bullock, or Lamb, or Goat. Male or Female.	He led the Offering to the Door of the Tabernacle, laid his hand upon it, killed it, opened it, took out Fat, Caul, and Kidneys and gave to the Priest to be burned	The Priest caught the Blood, sprinkled it around the Altar, and waved the "Breast" and "Right Shoulder" before the Lord.	All that was burned.	The "Wave Breast" and "Heave Shoulder".	The remainder of the Offering which he must eat with his Family or Friends in the Court of the Tabernacle. Deu. 12:5-12.	The "Reconciliation" The Offerer with G
SIN OFFERING	A Bullock, or Goat, (Male or Female), or Lamb according to the position of the Offerer.	He brought the Offering to the Door of the Tabernacle, laid his hand on it, slew it, removed the Fat, Kidneys and Caul and gave to the Priest to be burned on the Altar.	If for himself or Congregation, took of the Blood and sprinkled of it 7 times before the Veil, put of it on the Horns of the "Incense Altar" and poured the balance at the Foot of Burnt Offering Altar. If for others the Blood is put on the Horns and poured out at the Foot of the Burnt Offering Altar.	All of Priests' and Congregation's Offering that was not consumed on the Altar, was burned without the Camp.	All of the Offering of the Ruler or Common People, that was not burned on the Altar, belonged to the Priests, and was to be boiled and ate in the Court of the Tabernacle. Lev. 6:24-29.	Nothing	The Expiation of t Sin of the Offere
TRESPASS OFFERING	Female Lamb or Kid, Two Turtle Doves, or Two Young Pigeons, or 1/10 part of Ephah of Flour. It must contain no Oil or Frankincense.	Shall do as he did with the "Sin-Offering"	Shall do as he did with the "Sin-Offering" of the Common People.	All that was burned on the Altar.	What was not burned on the Altar belonged to the Priest	Nothing	Was to make Repa ation and Restitut for the Trespass c the Offerer.

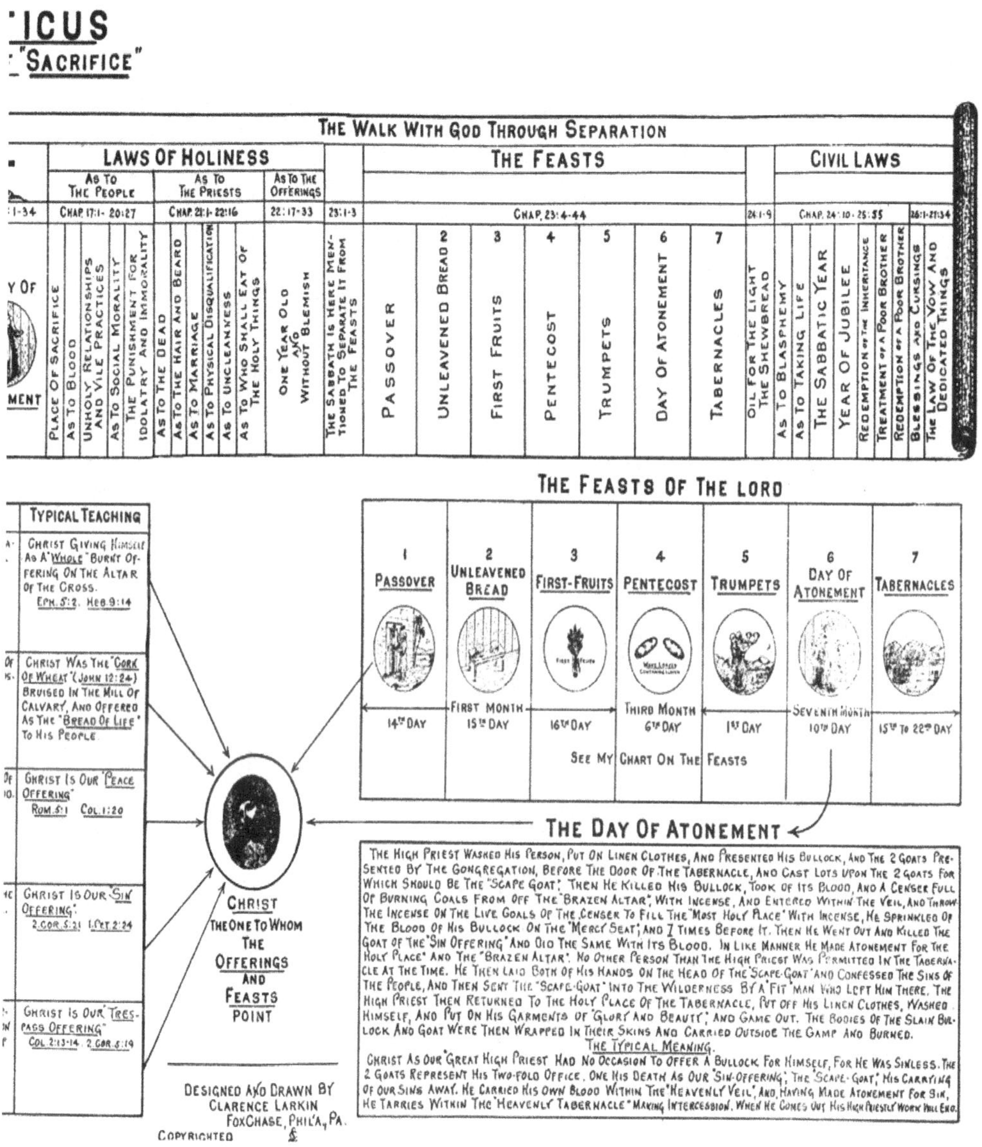

ICUS
"SACRIFICE"
THE WALK WITH GOD THROUGH SEPARATION
LAWS OF HOLINESS
AS TO THE PEOPLE
AS TO THE PRIESTS
AS TO THE OFFERINGS
THE FEASTS
CIVIL LAWS
CHAP. 17:1-20:27
CHAP. 21:1-22:16
22:17-33
23:1-3
CHAP. 23:4-44
24:1-9
CHAP. 24:10-25:55
26:1-27:34
PLACE OF SACRIFICE
AS TO BLOOD
UNHOLY RELATIONSHIPS AND VILE PRACTICES
AS TO SOCIAL MORALITY
THE PUNISHMENT FOR IDOLATRY AND IMMORALITY
AS TO THE DEAD
AS TO THE HAIR AND BEARD
AS TO MARRIAGE
AS TO PHYSICAL DISQUALIFICATION
AS TO UNCLEANNESS
AS TO WHO SHALL EAT OF THE HOLY THINGS
ONE YEAR OLD AND WITHOUT BLEMISH
THE SABBATH IS HERE MENTIONED TO SEPARATE IT FROM THE FEASTS
PASSOVER
2 UNLEAVENED BREAD
3 FIRST FRUITS
4 PENTECOST
5 TRUMPETS
6 DAY OF ATONEMENT
7 TABERNACLES
OIL FOR THE LIGHT THE SHEWBREAD
AS TO BLASPHEMY
AS TO TAKING LIFE
THE SABBATIC YEAR
YEAR OF JUBILEE
REDEMPTION OF THE INHERITANCE
TREATMENT OF A POOR BROTHER
REDEMPTION OF A POOR BROTHER
BLESSINGS AND CURSINGS
THE LAW OF THE VOW AND DEDICATED THINGS
Y OF
MENT
TYPICAL TEACHING
CHRIST GIVING HIMSELF AS A "WHOLE" BURNT OFFERING ON THE ALTAR OF THE CROSS. EPH. 5:2. HEB. 9:14
CHRIST WAS THE "CORN OF WHEAT" (JOHN 12:24) BRUISED IN THE MILL OF CALVARY, AND OFFERED AS THE "BREAD OF LIFE" TO HIS PEOPLE
CHRIST IS OUR "PEACE OFFERING" ROM. 5:1 COL. 1:20
CHRIST IS OUR "SIN OFFERING". 2 COR. 5:21 1 PET. 2:24
CHRIST IS OUR "TRESPASS OFFERING" COL. 2:13-14. 2 COR. 5:19
THE FEASTS OF THE LORD
1 PASSOVER
2 UNLEAVENED BREAD
3 FIRST-FRUITS
4 PENTECOST
5 TRUMPETS
6 DAY OF ATONEMENT
7 TABERNACLES
FIRST MONTH
THIRD MONTH
SEVENTH MONTH
14TH DAY
15TH DAY
16TH DAY
6TH DAY
1ST DAY
10TH DAY
15TH TO 22ND DAY
SEE MY CHART ON THE FEASTS
CHRIST THE ONE TO WHOM THE OFFERINGS AND FEASTS POINT
THE DAY OF ATONEMENT
THE HIGH PRIEST WASHED HIS PERSON, PUT ON LINEN CLOTHES, AND PRESENTED HIS BULLOCK, AND THE 2 GOATS PRESENTED BY THE CONGREGATION, BEFORE THE DOOR OF THE TABERNACLE, AND CAST LOTS UPON THE 2 GOATS FOR WHICH SHOULD BE THE "SCAPE GOAT". THEN HE KILLED HIS BULLOCK, TOOK OF ITS BLOOD, AND A CENSER FULL OF BURNING COALS FROM OFF THE "BRAZEN ALTAR", WITH INCENSE, AND ENTERED WITHIN THE VEIL, AND THREW THE INCENSE ON THE LIVE COALS OF THE CENSER TO FILL THE "MOST HOLY PLACE" WITH INCENSE, HE SPRINKLED OF THE BLOOD OF HIS BULLOCK ON THE "MERCY SEAT", AND 7 TIMES BEFORE IT. THEN HE WENT OUT AND KILLED THE GOAT OF THE "SIN OFFERING" AND DID THE SAME WITH ITS BLOOD. IN LIKE MANNER HE MADE ATONEMENT FOR THE "HOLY PLACE" AND THE "BRAZEN ALTAR". NO OTHER PERSON THAN THE HIGH PRIEST WAS PERMITTED IN THE TABERNACLE AT THE TIME. HE THEN LAID BOTH OF HIS HANDS ON THE HEAD OF THE "SCAPE-GOAT" AND CONFESSED THE SINS OF THE PEOPLE, AND THEN SENT THE "SCAPE-GOAT" INTO THE WILDERNESS BY A "FIT" MAN WHO LEFT HIM THERE. THE HIGH PRIEST THEN RETURNED TO THE HOLY PLACE OF THE TABERNACLE, PUT OFF HIS LINEN CLOTHES, WASHED HIMSELF, AND PUT ON HIS GARMENTS OF "GLORY AND BEAUTY", AND CAME OUT. THE BODIES OF THE SLAIN BULLOCK AND GOAT WERE THEN WRAPPED IN THEIR SKINS AND CARRIED OUTSIDE THE CAMP AND BURNED.
THE TYPICAL MEANING.
CHRIST AS OUR "GREAT HIGH PRIEST" HAD NO OCCASION TO OFFER A BULLOCK FOR HIMSELF, FOR HE WAS SINLESS. THE 2 GOATS REPRESENT HIS TWO-FOLD OFFICE. ONE HIS DEATH AS OUR "SIN-OFFERING", THE "SCAPE-GOAT" HIS CARRYING OF OUR SINS AWAY. HE CARRIED HIS OWN BLOOD WITHIN THE "HEAVENLY VEIL", AND, HAVING MADE ATONEMENT FOR SIN, HE TARRIES WITHIN THE "HEAVENLY TABERNACLE" MAKING INTERCESSION. WHEN HE COMES OUT HIS HIGH PRIESTLY WORK WILL END.
DESIGNED AND DRAWN BY CLARENCE LARKIN FOXCHASE, PHIL'A, PA.
COPYRIGHTED

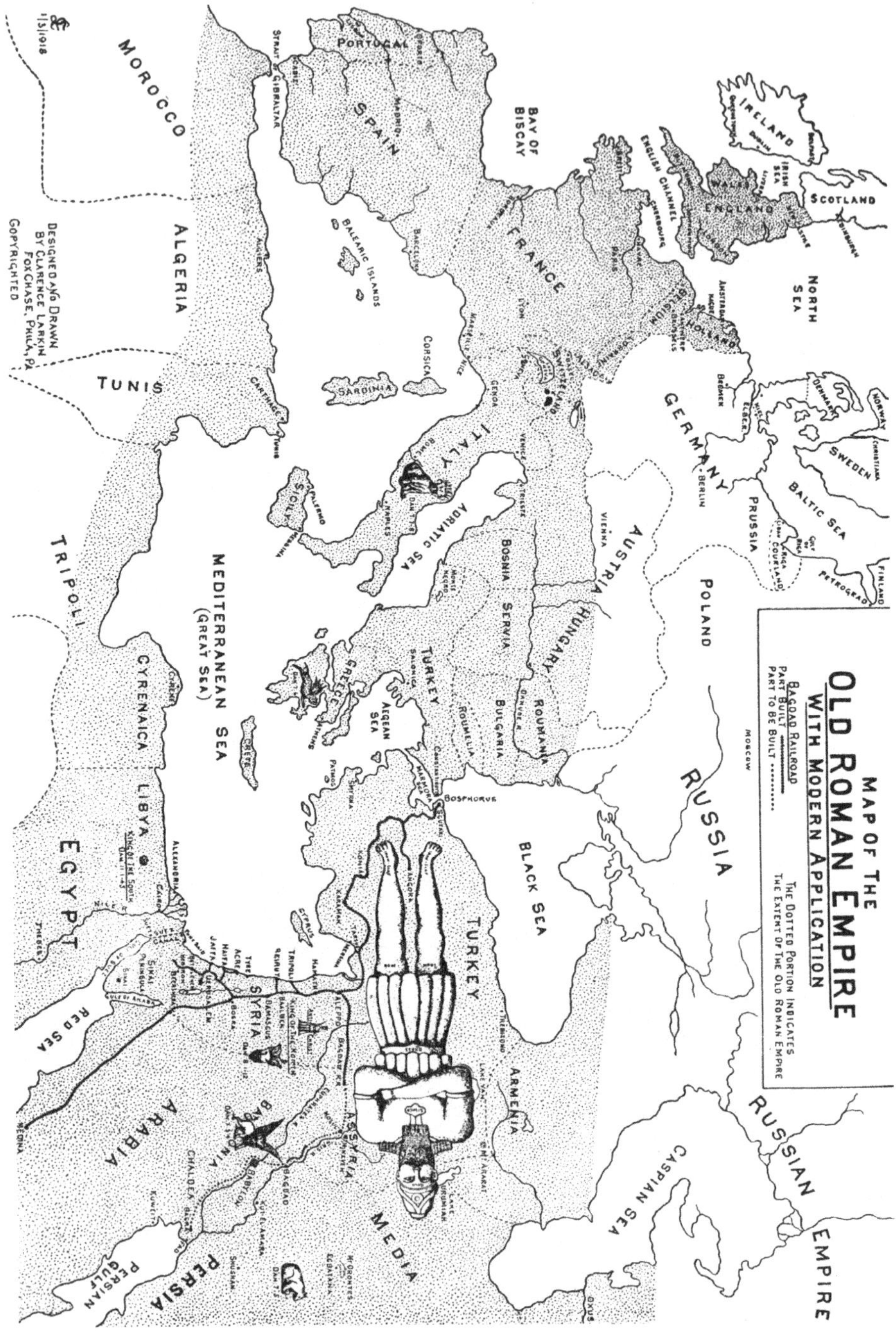
MAP OF THE
OLD ROMAN EMPIRE
WITH MODERN APPLICATION
BAGDAD RAILROAD
PART BUILT
PART TO BE BUILT
THE DOTTED PORTION INDICATES
THE EXTENT OF THE OLD ROMAN EMPIRE
DESIGNED AND DRAWN
BY CLARENCE LARKIN
FOX CHASE, PHILA. PA.
COPYRIGHTED
1/3/1918
MOROCCO
ALGERIA
TUNIS
TRIPOLI
CYRENAICA
LIBYA
EGYPT
PORTUGAL
SPAIN
STRAIT OF GIBRALTAR
BAY OF BISCAY
BALEARIC ISLANDS
CORSICA
SARDINIA
SICILY
ITALY
ADRIATIC SEA
FRANCE
IRELAND
SCOTLAND
ENGLAND
WALES
ENGLISH CHANNEL
NORTH SEA
BELGIUM
HOLLAND
SWITZERLAND
GERMANY
DENMARK
NORWAY
SWEDEN
BALTIC SEA
PRUSSIA
FINLAND
PETROGRAD
AUSTRIA
HUNGARY
POLAND
RUSSIA
MOSCOW
BOSNIA
SERVIA
ROUMANIA
BULGARIA
ROUMELIA
TURKEY
GREECE
AEGEAN SEA
CRETE
MEDITERRANEAN SEA
(GREAT SEA)
BOSPHORUS
BLACK SEA
ARMENIA
SYRIA
ASSYRIA
BABYLONIA
CHALDEA
MEDIA
PERSIA
PERSIAN GULF
ARABIA
RED SEA
CASPIAN SEA
RUSSIAN EMPIRE
CYPRUS
ALEXANDRIA
MEDINA

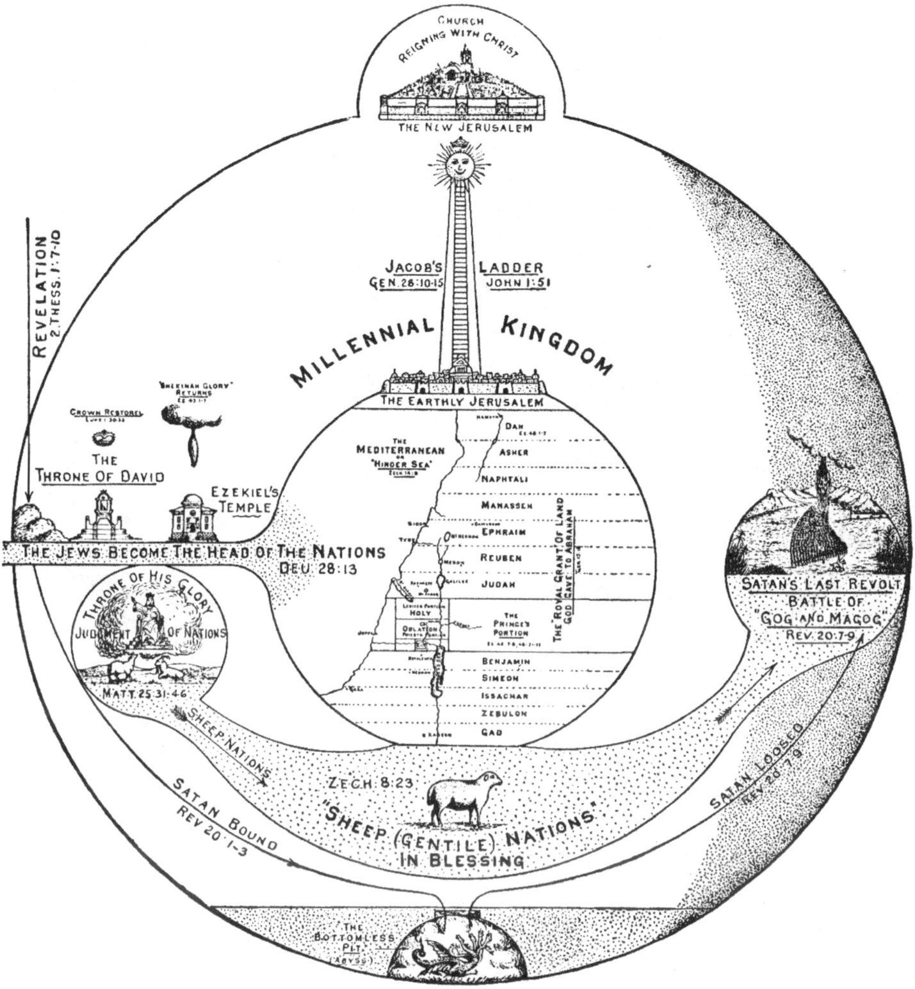

MESSIANIC DISPENSATION
(RIGHTEOUSNESS)

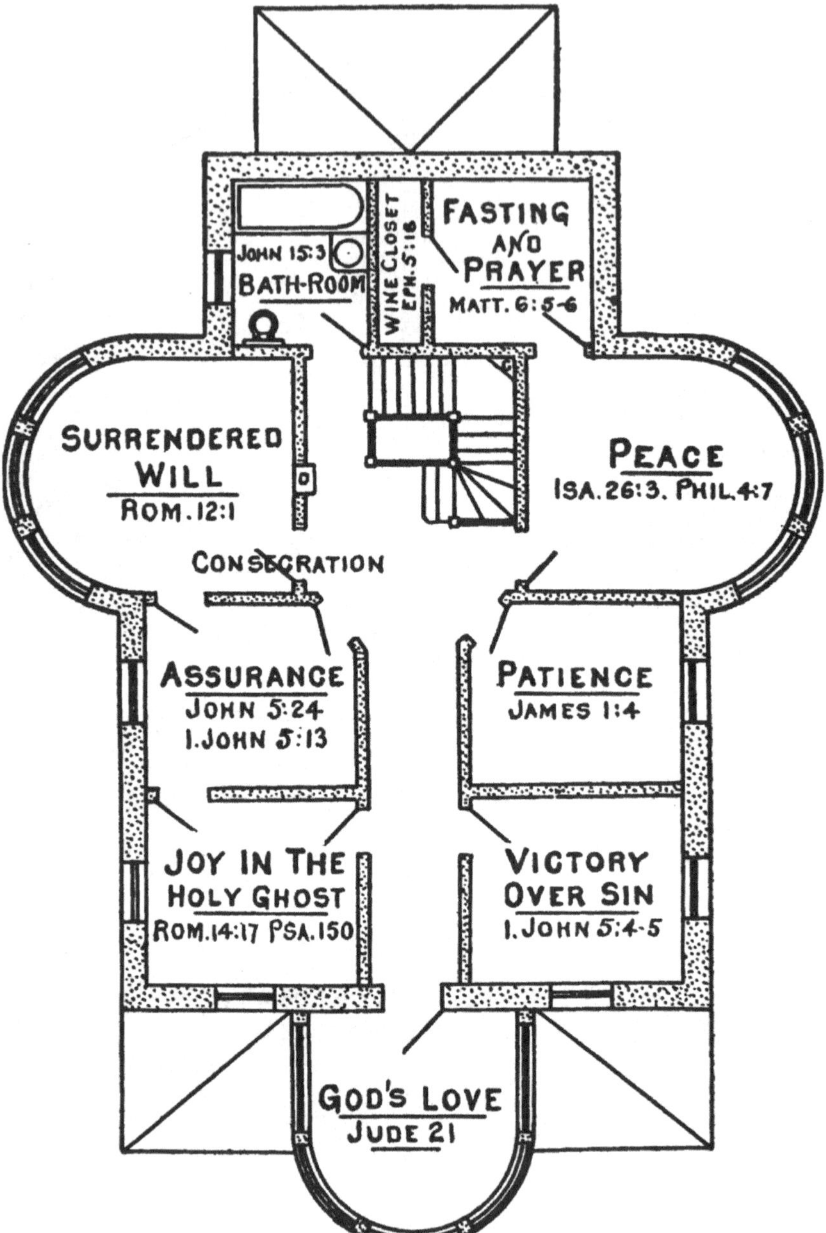

PALACE BEAUTIFUL - SECOND FLOOR PLAN

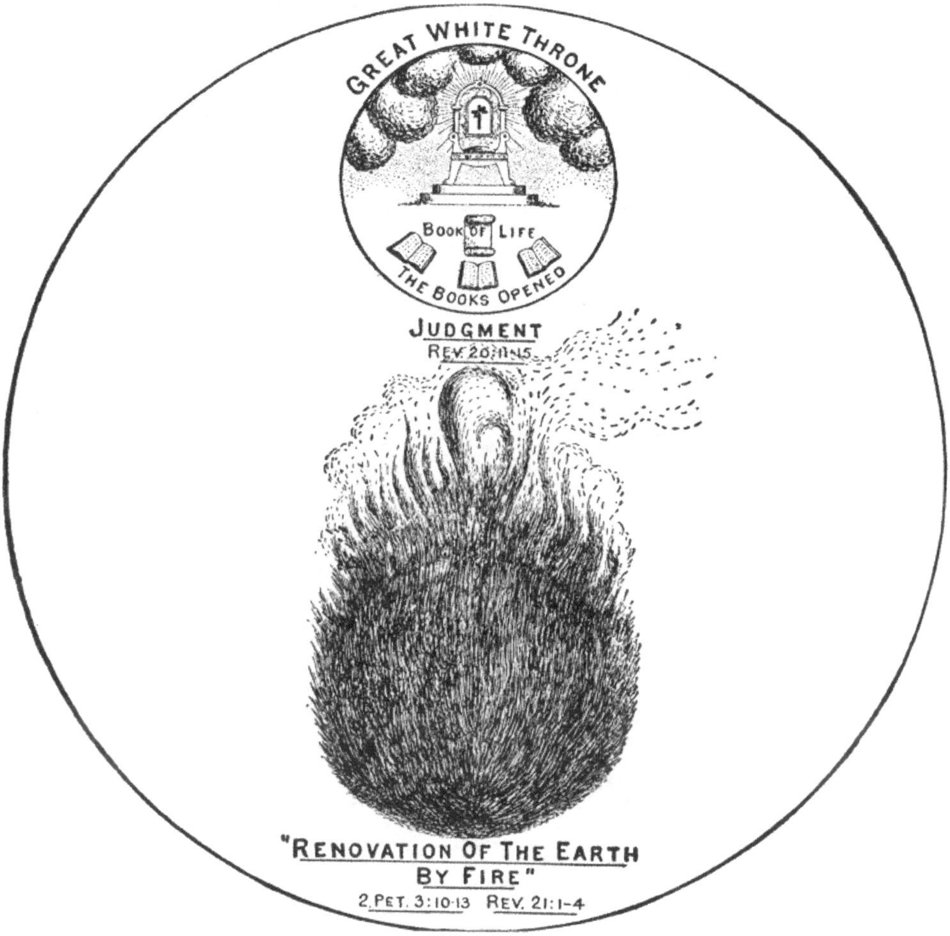

PARENTHETICAL DISPENSATION
BETWEEN
THE MILLENNIUM AND THE NEW EARTH

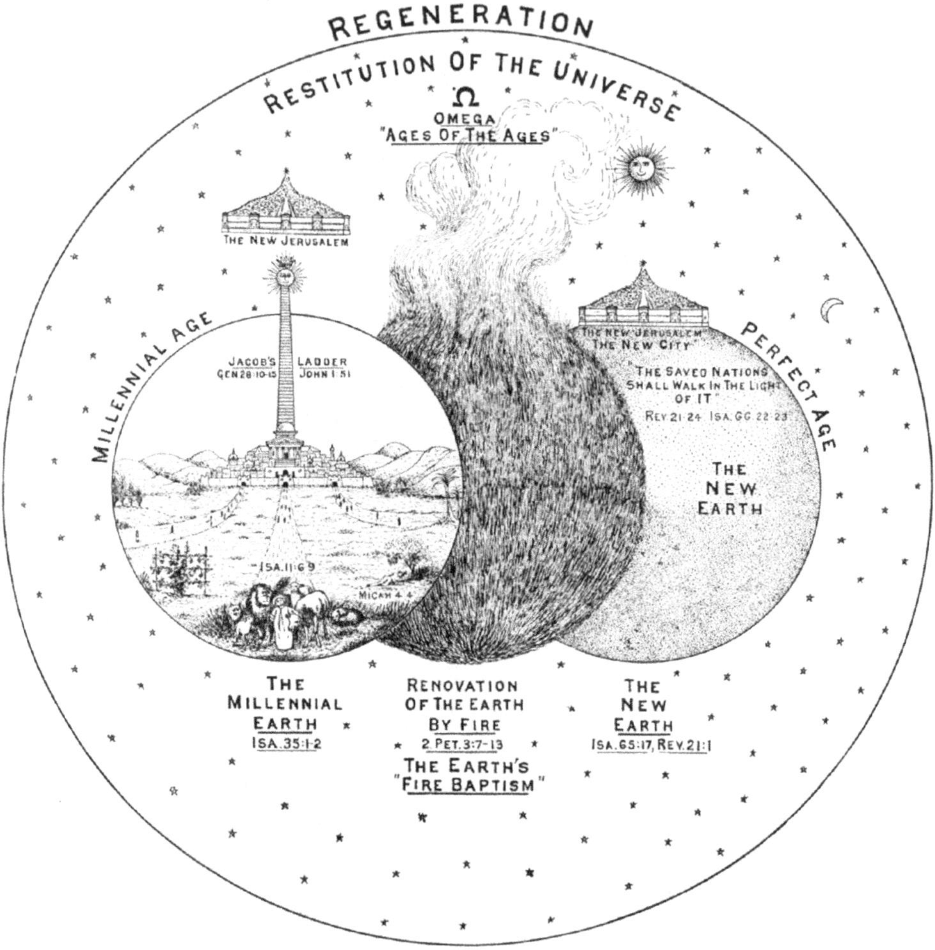

REGENERATION
RESTITUTION OF THE UNIVERSE
Ω
OMEGA
"AGES OF THE AGES"
THE NEW JERUSALEM
MILLENNIAL AGE
JACOB'S LADDER
GEN 28:10-15 JOHN 1:51
ISA. 11:6-9
MICAH 4:4
THE NEW JERUSALEM
"THE NEW CITY"
PERFECT AGE
"THE SAVED NATIONS SHALL WALK IN THE LIGHT OF IT"
REV 21:24 ISA. GG 22:23
THE NEW EARTH
THE MILLENNIAL EARTH
ISA. 35:1-2
RENOVATION OF THE EARTH BY FIRE
2 PET. 3:7-13
THE EARTH'S "FIRE BAPTISM"
THE NEW EARTH
ISA. 65:17, REV. 21:1

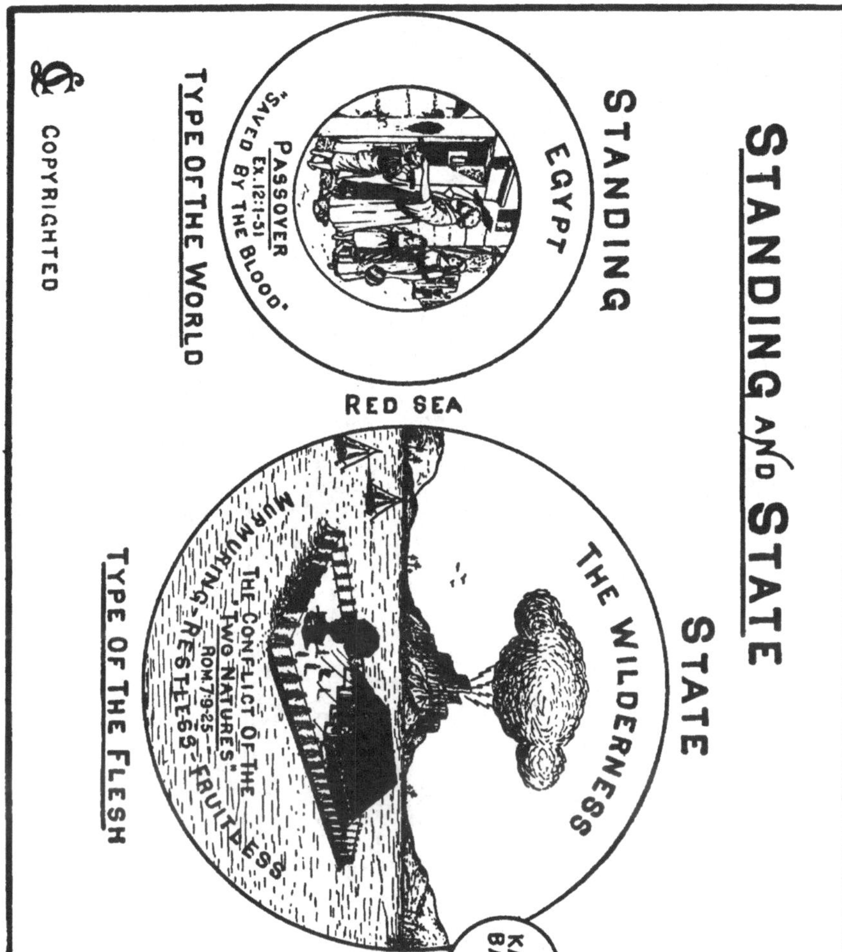
STANDING AND STATE
STANDING
EGYPT
PASSOVER
EX. 12:1-51
"SAVED BY THE BLOOD"
TYPE OF THE WORLD
COPYRIGHTED
RED SEA
STATE
THE WILDERNESS
THE CONFLICT OF THE "TWO NATURES"
ROM. 7:9-25
MURMURING - RESTLESS - FRUITLESS
TYPE OF THE FLESH
JORDAN
KADESH BARNEA
EXPERIENCE
CANAAN
"GRAPES OF ESHCOL"
NUM. 14:21-25
"THE REST OF FAITH"
TYPE OF THE DEVIL
DESIGNED AND DRAWN
BY CLARENCE LARKIN
FOXCHASE, PHILA, PA.

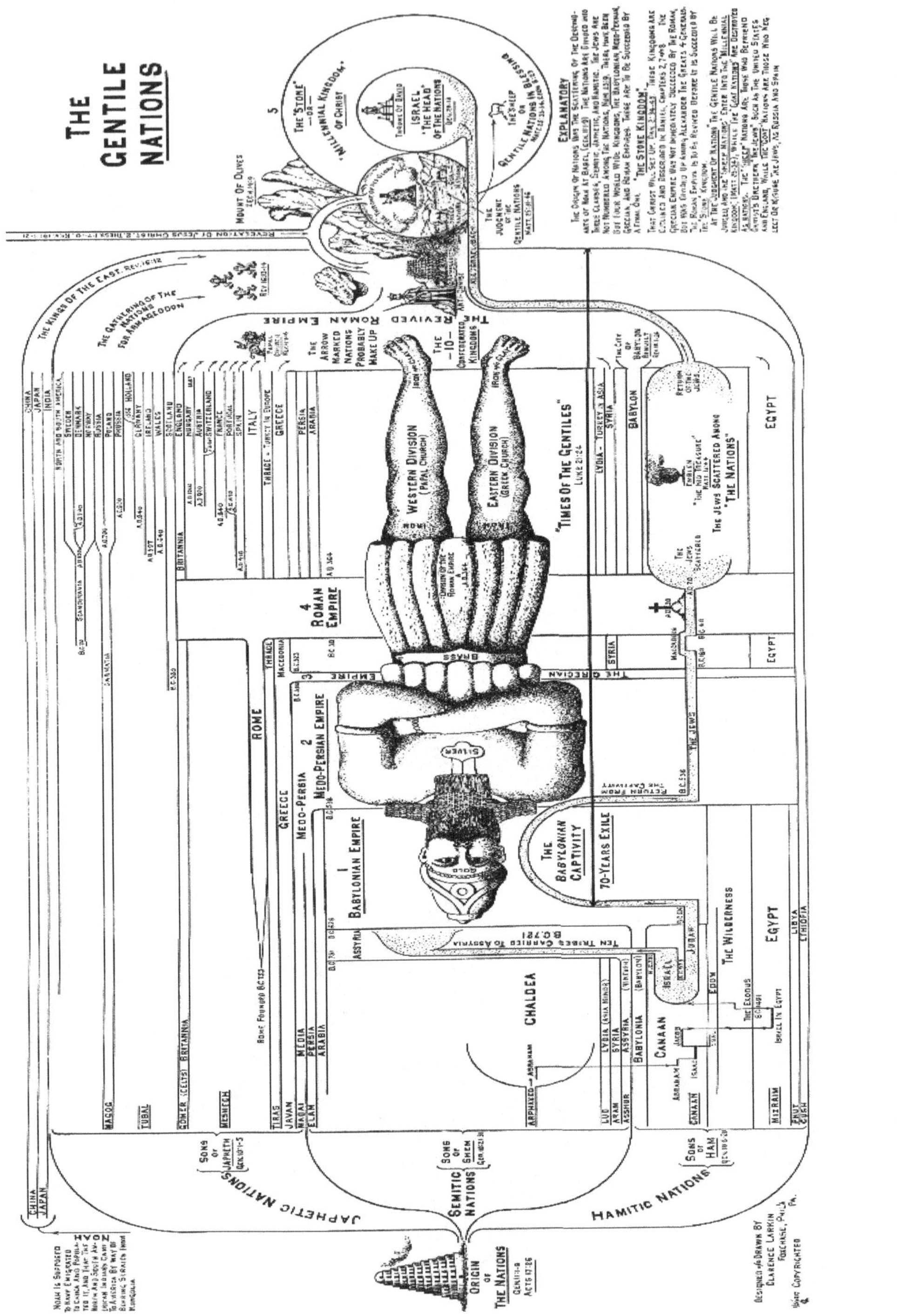
THE GENTILE NATIONS
"TIMES OF THE GENTILES"
BABYLONIAN EMPIRE
MEDO-PERSIAN EMPIRE
ROMAN EMPIRE
THE REVIVED ROMAN EMPIRE
WESTERN DIVISION (PAPAL CHURCH)
EASTERN DIVISION (GREEK CHURCH)
THE BABYLONIAN CAPTIVITY
70-YEARS EXILE
JAPHETIC NATIONS
SEMITIC NATIONS
HAMITIC NATIONS
CHALDEA
EGYPT
BABYLON
ROME
GREECE
ITALY
EXPLANATORY

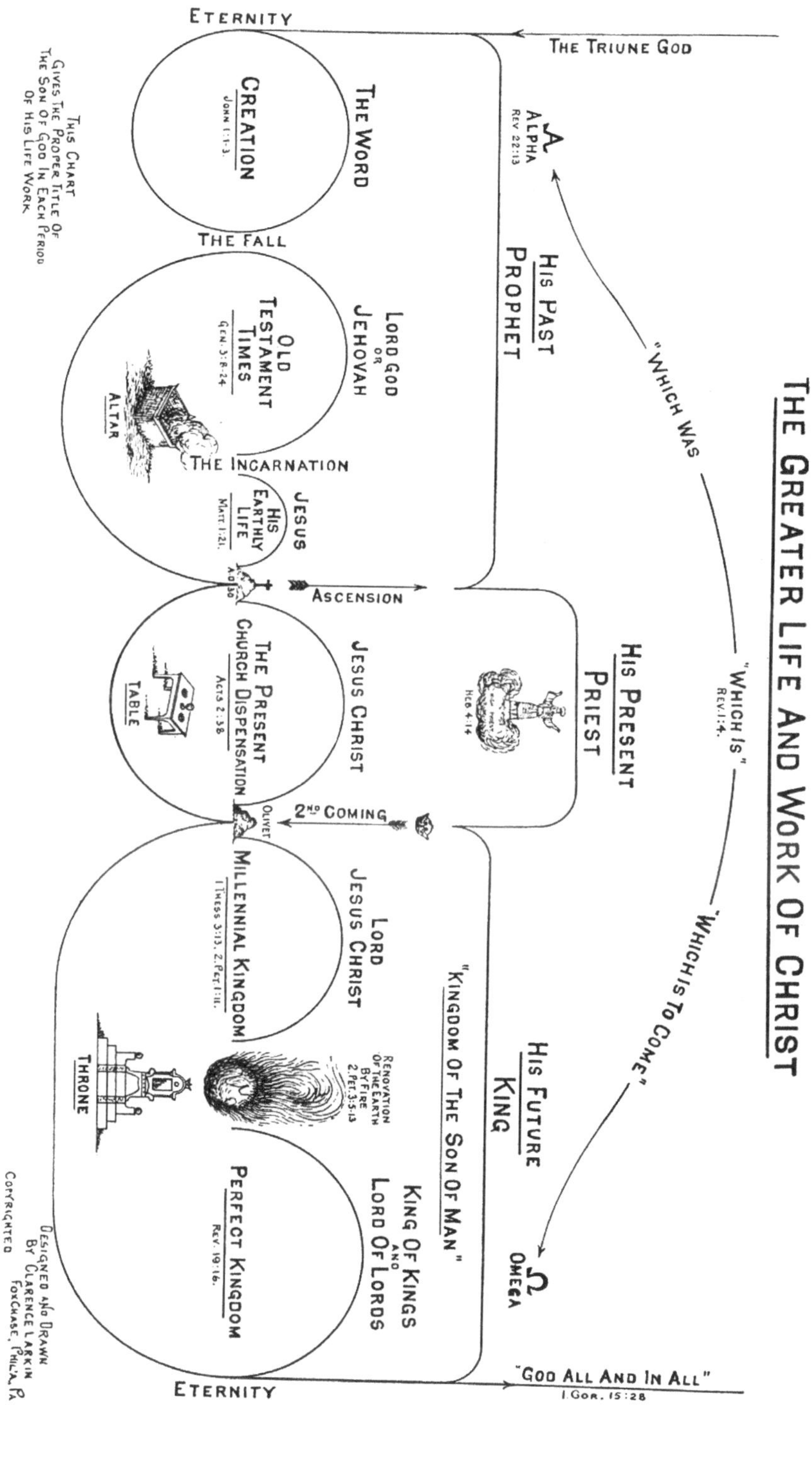
The Greater Life And Work Of Christ
Eternity
The Triune God
A
Alpha
Rev 22:13
"Which Was
His Past
Prophet
The Word
Creation
John 1:1-3.
The Fall
Lord God or Jehovah
Old Testament Times
Gen. 3:8-24
Altar
The Incarnation
Jesus
His Earthly Life
Matt 1:21.
A.D. 30
Ascension
His Present
Priest
Heb 4:14
"Which Is"
Rev. 1:4.
Jesus Christ
The Present Church Dispensation
Acts 2:38.
Table
2nd Coming
Olivet
Lord Jesus Christ
Millennial Kingdom
1 Thess 3:13. 2 Pet 1:11.
"Which Is To Come"
"Kingdom Of The Son Of Man"
His Future
King
Renovation Of The Earth By Fire
2 Pet. 3:5-13
Throne
King Of Kings and Lord Of Lords
Perfect Kingdom
Rev. 19:16.
Ω
Omega
Eternity
"God All And In All"
1 Cor. 15:28
This Chart Gives The Proper Title Of The Son Of God In Each Period Of His Life Work
Designed and Drawn By Clarence Larkin Foxchase, Phil'a, Pa
Copyrighted

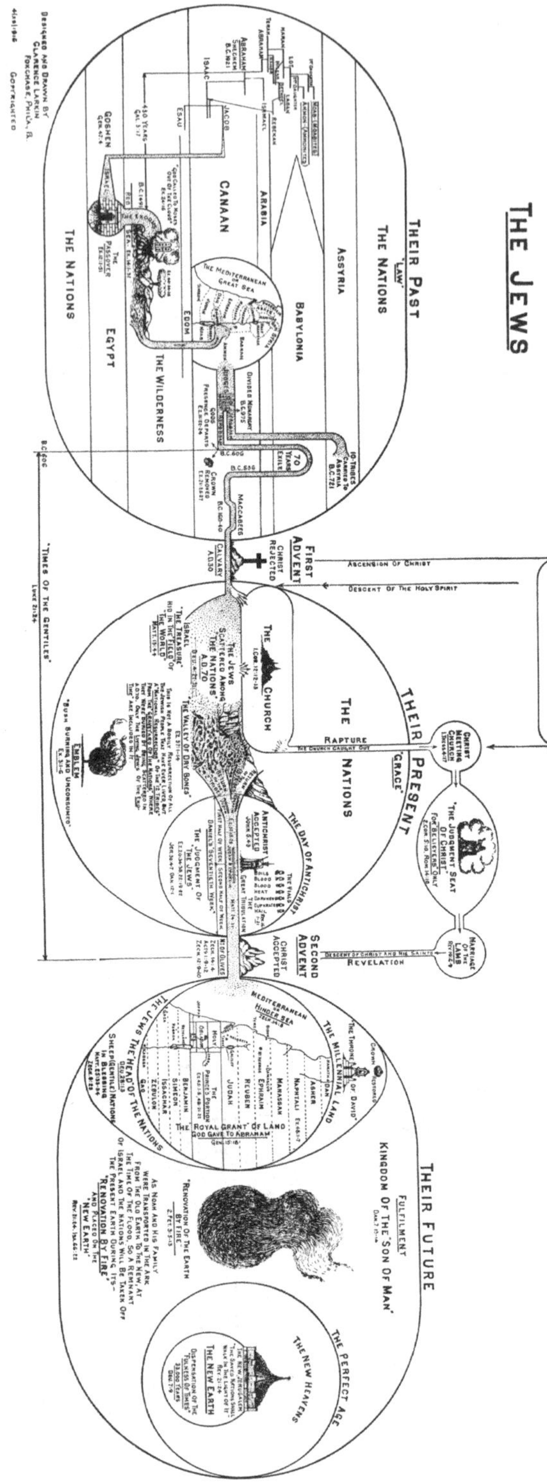
THE JEWS
THEIR PAST
"LAW"
THE NATIONS
ASSYRIA
BABYLONIA
ARABIA
CANAAN
THE MEDITERRANEAN OR GREAT SEA
EDOM
EGYPT
THE WILDERNESS
GOSHEN
ESAU
JACOB
ISAAC
ABRAHAM
THE NATIONS
FIRST ADVENT
CHRIST REJECTED
CALVARY A.D. 30
MACCABEES
ASCENSION OF CHRIST
DESCENT OF THE HOLY SPIRIT
PRIESTHOOD OF CHRIST
THEIR PRESENT
"GRACE"
THE NATIONS
THE CHURCH
RAPTURE
THE CHURCH CAUGHT OUT
CHRIST MEETING CHURCH
THE JEWS SCATTERED AMONG "THE NATIONS" A.D. 70
"THE VALLEY OF DRY BONES"
THE DAY OF ANTICHRIST
ANTICHRIST ACCEPTED
"THE JUDGMENT SEAT OF CHRIST"
MARRIAGE OF THE LAMB
SECOND ADVENT
CHRIST ACCEPTED
REVELATION
"TIMES OF THE GENTILES"
EMBLEM
"BUSH BURNING AND UNCONSUMED"
THEIR FUTURE
FULFILMENT
KINGDOM OF THE "SON OF MAN"
THE MILLENNIAL LAND
THE ROYAL GRANT OF LAND GOD GAVE TO ABRAHAM
THE JEWS THE "HEAD" OF THE NATIONS
"RENOVATION OF THE EARTH BY FIRE"
THE PERFECT AGE
THE NEW HEAVENS
THE NEW EARTH
DESIGNED AND DRAWN BY CLARENCE LARKIN FOX CHASE, PHILA. PA.
COPYRIGHTED

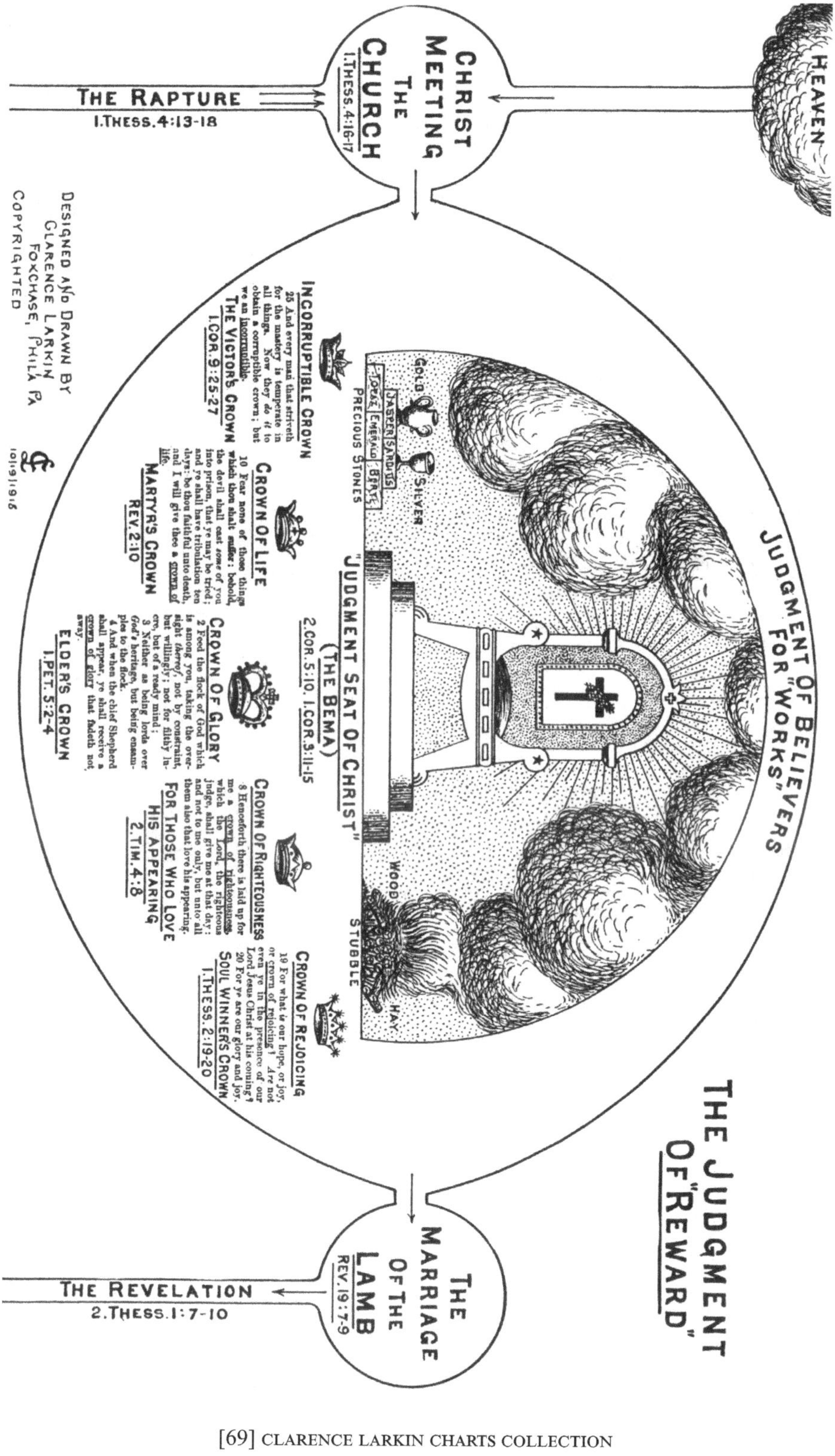
HEAVEN
CHRIST MEETING THE CHURCH
1.THESS.4:16-17
THE RAPTURE
1.THESS.4:13-18
JUDGMENT OF BELIEVERS FOR "WORKS"
THE JUDGMENT OF "REWARD"
GOLD
SILVER
PRECIOUS STONES
JASPER SARDIUS TOPAZ EMERALD BERYL
WOOD
HAY
STUBBLE
"JUDGMENT SEAT OF CHRIST"
(THE BEMA)
2.COR.5:10. 1.COR.3:11-15
INCORRUPTIBLE CROWN
25 And every man that striveth for the mastery is temperate in all things. Now they do it to obtain a corruptible crown; but we an incorruptible.
THE VICTOR'S CROWN
1.COR.9:25-27
CROWN OF LIFE
10 Fear none of those things which thou shalt suffer: behold, the devil shall cast some of you into prison, that ye may be tried; and ye shall have tribulation ten days: be thou faithful unto death, and I will give thee a crown of life.
MARTYR'S CROWN
REV.2:10
CROWN OF GLORY
2 Feed the flock of God which is among you, taking the oversight thereof, not by constraint, but willingly; not for filthy lucre, but of a ready mind;
3 Neither as being lords over God's heritage, but being ensamples to the flock.
4 And when the chief Shepherd shall appear, ye shall receive a crown of glory that fadeth not away.
ELDER'S CROWN
1.PET.5:2-4
CROWN OF RIGHTEOUSNESS
8 Henceforth there is laid up for me a crown of righteousness, which the Lord, the righteous judge, shall give me at that day: and not to me only, but unto all them also that love his appearing.
FOR THOSE WHO LOVE HIS APPEARING
2.TIM.4:8
CROWN OF REJOICING
19 For what is our hope, or joy, or crown of rejoicing? Are not even ye in the presence of our Lord Jesus Christ at his coming?
20 For ye are our glory and joy.
SOUL WINNER'S CROWN
1.THESS.2:19-20
THE MARRIAGE OF THE LAMB
REV.19:7-9
THE REVELATION
2.THESS.1:7-10
DESIGNED AND DRAWN BY
CLARENCE LARKIN
FOXCHASE, PHILA PA
COPYRIGHTED
CL
1019/1916

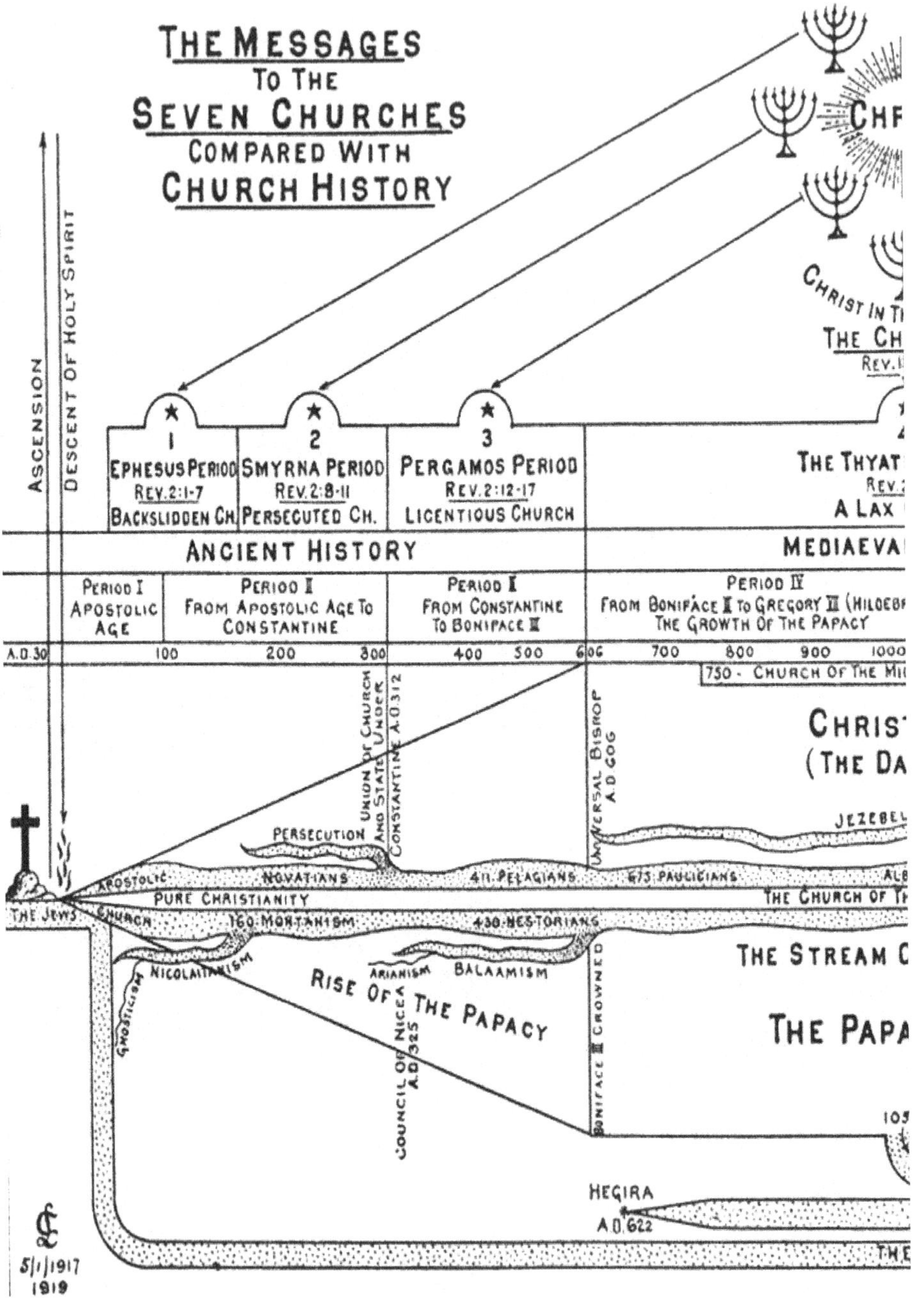
THE MESSAGES
TO THE
SEVEN CHURCHES
COMPARED WITH
CHURCH HISTORY
ASCENSION
DESCENT OF HOLY SPIRIT
1
EPHESUS PERIOD
REV. 2:1-7
BACKSLIDDEN CH.
2
SMYRNA PERIOD
REV. 2:8-11
PERSECUTED CH.
3
PERGAMOS PERIOD
REV. 2:12-17
LICENTIOUS CHURCH
THE THYAT
A LAX
THE CH
ANCIENT HISTORY
MEDIAEVA
PERIOD I
APOSTOLIC AGE
PERIOD II
FROM APOSTOLIC AGE TO CONSTANTINE
PERIOD III
FROM CONSTANTINE TO BONIFACE III
PERIOD IV
FROM BONIFACE III TO GREGORY VII (HILDEB
THE GROWTH OF THE PAPACY
A.D. 30
100
200
300
400
500
606
700
800
900
1000
750 - CHURCH OF THE MI
UNION OF CHURCH AND STATE UNDER CONSTANTINE A.D. 312
UNIVERSAL BISHOP A.D. 606
CHRIS
(THE DA
PERSECUTION
JEZEBEL
APOSTOLIC
NOVATIANS
411 PELAGIANS
673 PAULICIANS
PURE CHRISTIANITY
THE CHURCH OF TH
THE JEWS
CHURCH
160 MONTANISM
430 NESTORIANS
NICOLAITANISM
GNOSTICISM
ARIANISM
BALAAMISM
RISE OF THE PAPACY
COUNCIL OF NICEA A.D. 325
BONIFACE III CROWNED
THE STREAM
THE PAPA
HEGIRA
A.D. 622
5/1/1917
1919

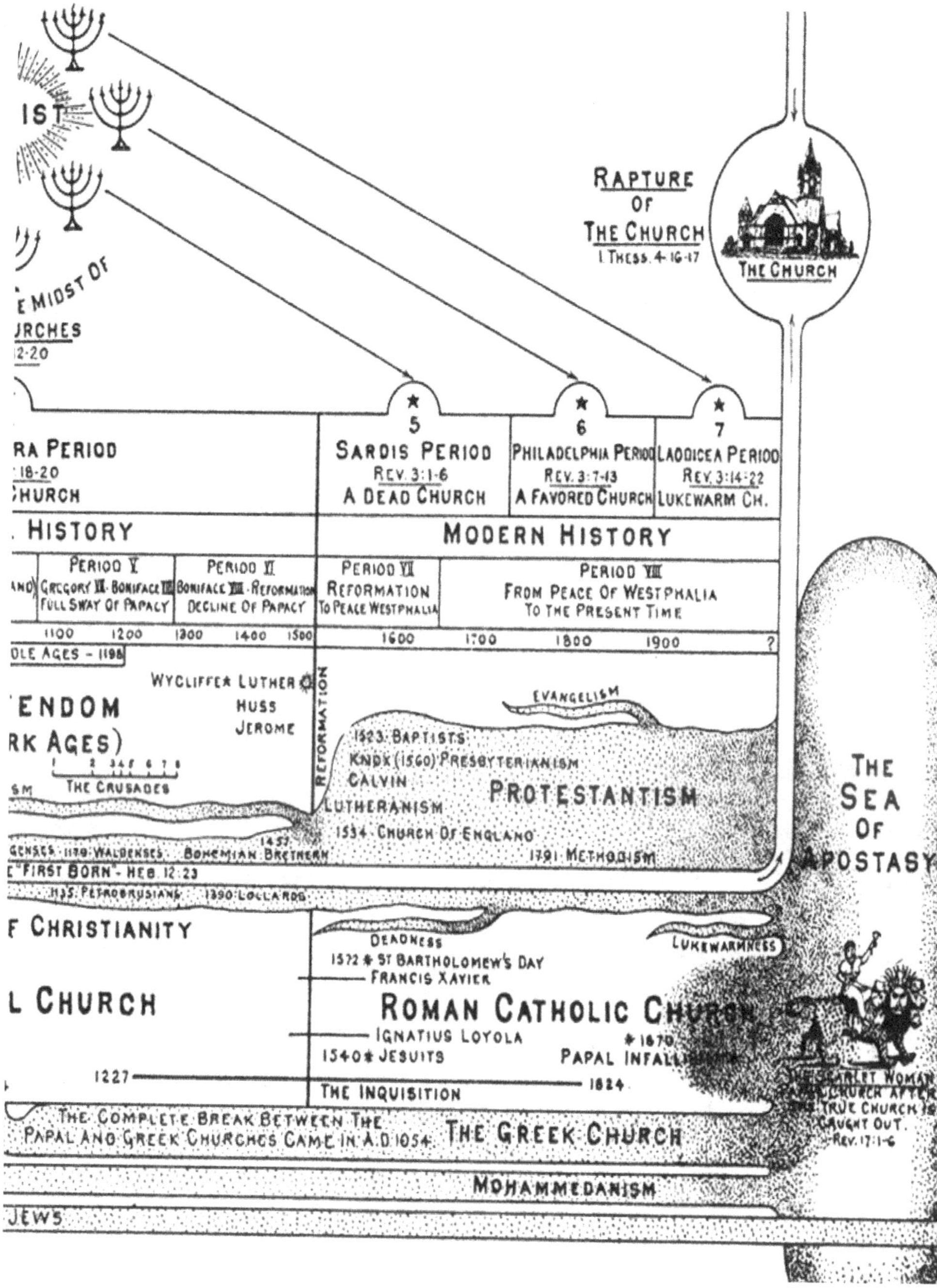
RAPTURE OF THE CHURCH
I THESS. 4-16-17
THE CHURCH
5
SARDIS PERIOD
REV. 3:1-6
A DEAD CHURCH
6
PHILADELPHIA PERIOD
REV. 3:7-13
A FAVORED CHURCH
7
LAODICEA PERIOD
REV. 3:14-22
LUKEWARM CH.
HISTORY
MODERN HISTORY
PERIOD V
GREGORY VII - BONIFACE VIII
FULL SWAY OF PAPACY
PERIOD VI
BONIFACE VIII - REFORMATION
DECLINE OF PAPACY
PERIOD VII
REFORMATION
TO PEACE WESTPHALIA
PERIOD VIII
FROM PEACE OF WESTPHALIA
TO THE PRESENT TIME
1100 1200 1300 1400 1500 1600 1700 1800 1900 ?
WYCLIFFE LUTHER
HUSS
JEROME
THE CRUSADES
REFORMATION
EVANGELISM
1523 BAPTISTS
KNOX (1560) PRESBYTERIANISM
CALVIN
LUTHERANISM
PROTESTANTISM
1534 CHURCH OF ENGLAND
1791 METHODISM
1457
1170 WALDENSES
BOHEMIAN BRETHREN
"FIRST BORN" - HEB. 12:23
1135 PETROBRUSIANS
1390 LOLLARDS
CHRISTIANITY
DEADNESS
1572 ST BARTHOLOMEW'S DAY
FRANCIS XAVIER
LUKEWARMNESS
CHURCH
ROMAN CATHOLIC CHURCH
IGNATIUS LOYOLA
1540 JESUITS
1870
PAPAL INFALLIBILITY
1227
1824
THE INQUISITION
THE SEA OF APOSTASY
THE SCARLET WOMAN
PAPAL CHURCH AFTER THE TRUE CHURCH IS CAUGHT OUT.
REV. 17:1-6
THE COMPLETE BREAK BETWEEN THE PAPAL AND GREEK CHURCHES CAME IN A.D. 1054.
THE GREEK CHURCH
MOHAMMEDANISM
JEWS

THE MYSTERIES

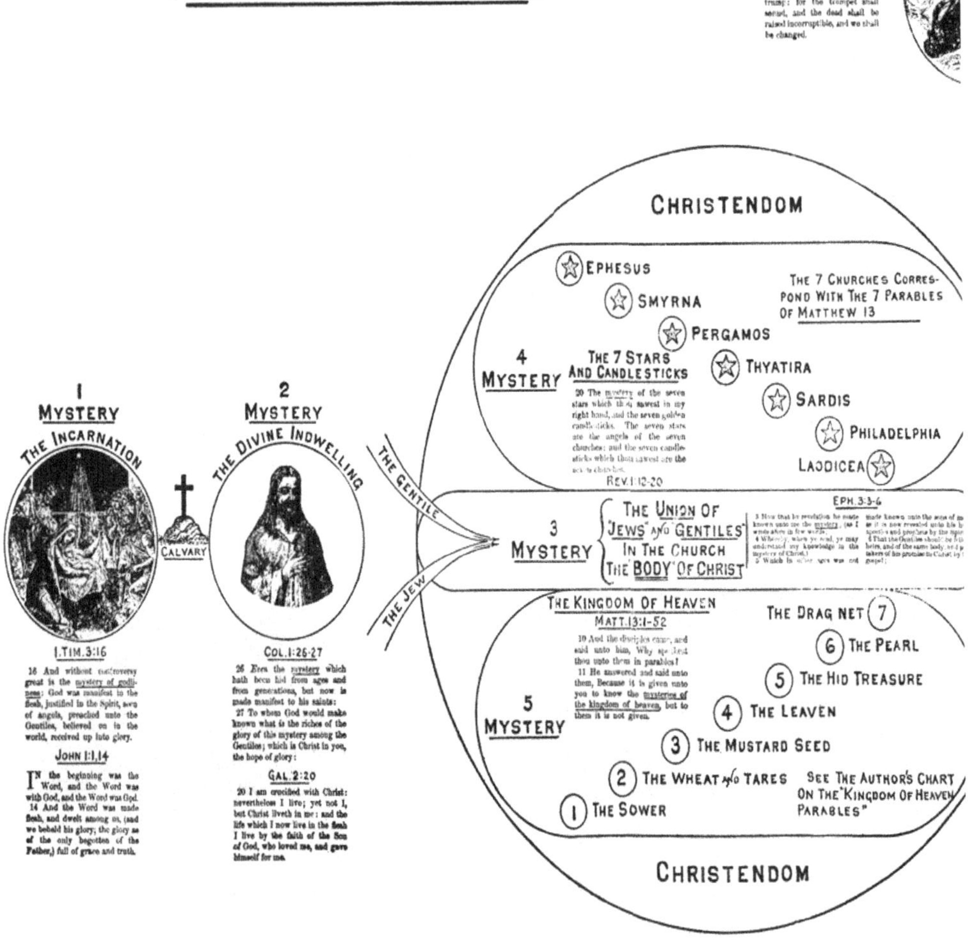

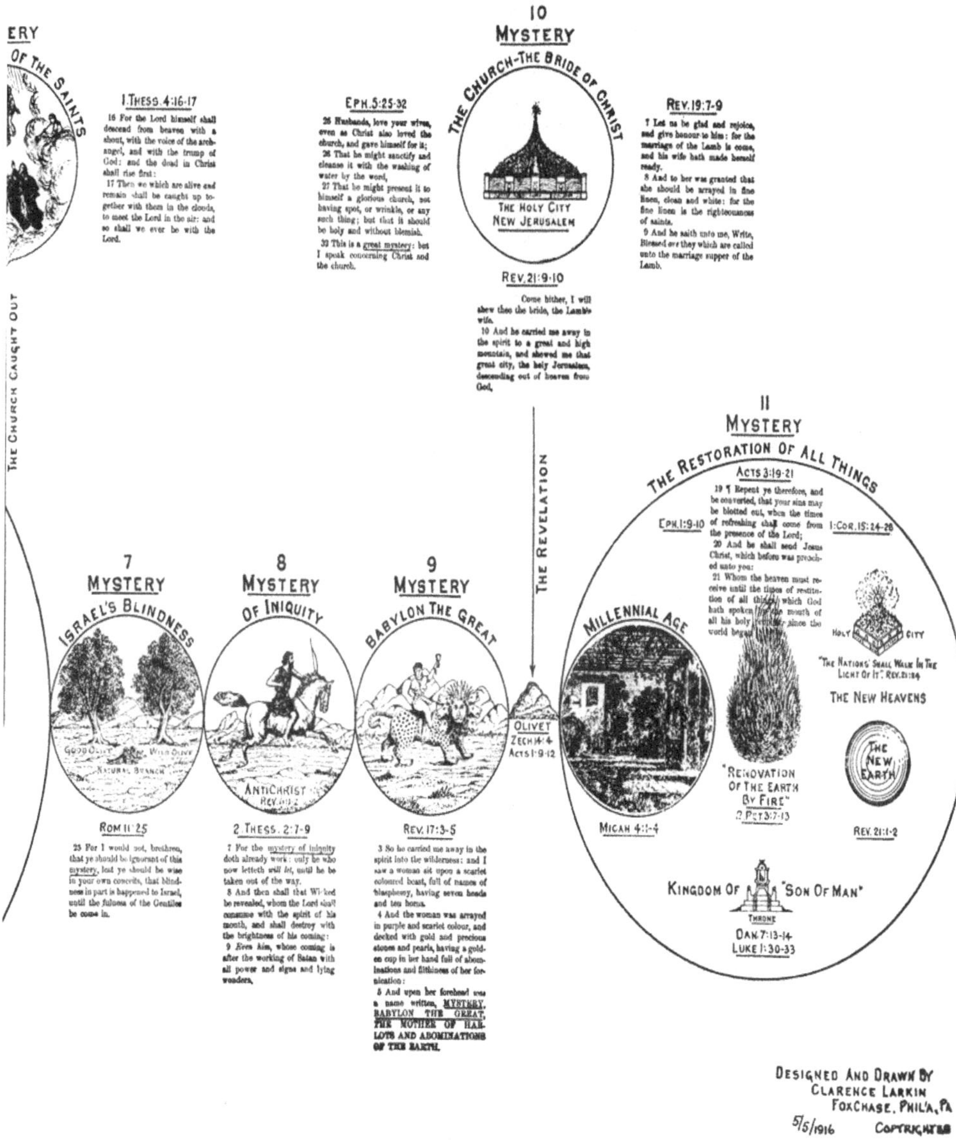

ERY
OF THE SAINTS
THE CHURCH CAUGHT OUT
I.THESS.4:16-17
16 For the Lord himself shall descend from heaven with a shout, with the voice of the archangel, and with the trump of God: and the dead in Christ shall rise first:
17 Then we which are alive and remain shall be caught up together with them in the clouds, to meet the Lord in the air: and so shall we ever be with the Lord.
10
MYSTERY
THE CHURCH-THE BRIDE OF CHRIST
EPH.5:25-32
25 Husbands, love your wives, even as Christ also loved the church, and gave himself for it;
26 That he might sanctify and cleanse it with the washing of water by the word,
27 That he might present it to himself a glorious church, not having spot, or wrinkle, or any such thing; but that it should be holy and without blemish.
32 This is a great mystery: but I speak concerning Christ and the church.
THE HOLY CITY
NEW JERUSALEM
REV.19:7-9
7 Let us be glad and rejoice, and give honour to him: for the marriage of the Lamb is come, and his wife hath made herself ready.
8 And to her was granted that she should be arrayed in fine linen, clean and white: for the fine linen is the righteousness of saints.
9 And he saith unto me, Write, Blessed are they which are called unto the marriage supper of the Lamb.
REV.21:9-10
Come hither, I will shew thee the bride, the Lamb's wife.
10 And he carried me away in the spirit to a great and high mountain, and shewed me that great city, the holy Jerusalem, descending out of heaven from God,
THE REVELATION
7
MYSTERY
ISRAEL'S BLINDNESS
GOOD OLIVE
WILD OLIVE
NATURAL BRANCH
ROM 11:25
25 For I would not, brethren, that ye should be ignorant of this mystery, lest ye should be wise in your own conceits, that blindness in part is happened to Israel, until the fulness of the Gentiles be come in.
8
MYSTERY
OF INIQUITY
ANTICHRIST
2 THESS. 2:7-9
7 For the mystery of iniquity doth already work: only he who now letteth will let, until he be taken out of the way.
8 And then shall that Wicked be revealed, whom the Lord shall consume with the spirit of his mouth, and shall destroy with the brightness of his coming:
9 Even him, whose coming is after the working of Satan with all power and signs and lying wonders,
9
MYSTERY
BABYLON THE GREAT
REV.17:3-5
3 So he carried me away in the spirit into the wilderness: and I saw a woman sit upon a scarlet coloured beast, full of names of blasphemy, having seven heads and ten horns.
4 And the woman was arrayed in purple and scarlet colour, and decked with gold and precious stones and pearls, having a golden cup in her hand full of abominations and filthiness of her fornication:
5 And upon her forehead was a name written, MYSTERY, BABYLON THE GREAT, THE MOTHER OF HARLOTS AND ABOMINATIONS OF THE EARTH.
OLIVET
ZECH.14:4
ACTS 1:9-12
11
MYSTERY
THE RESTORATION OF ALL THINGS
ACTS 3:19-21
19 ¶ Repent ye therefore, and be converted, that your sins may be blotted out, when the times of refreshing shall come from the presence of the Lord;
20 And he shall send Jesus Christ, which before was preached unto you:
21 Whom the heaven must receive until the times of restitution of all things, which God hath spoken by the mouth of all his holy prophets since the world began.
EPH.1:9-10
1:COR.15:24-28
MILLENNIAL AGE
HOLY CITY
"THE NATIONS SHALL WALK IN THE LIGHT OF IT". REV.21:24
THE NEW HEAVENS
THE NEW EARTH
"RENOVATION OF THE EARTH BY FIRE"
2 PET.3:7-13
MICAH 4:1-4
REV.21:1-2
KINGDOM OF "SON OF MAN"
THRONE
DAN.7:13-14
LUKE 1:30-33
DESIGNED AND DRAWN BY
CLARENCE LARKIN
FOXCHASE, PHIL'A, PA
5/5/1916
COPYRIGHTED

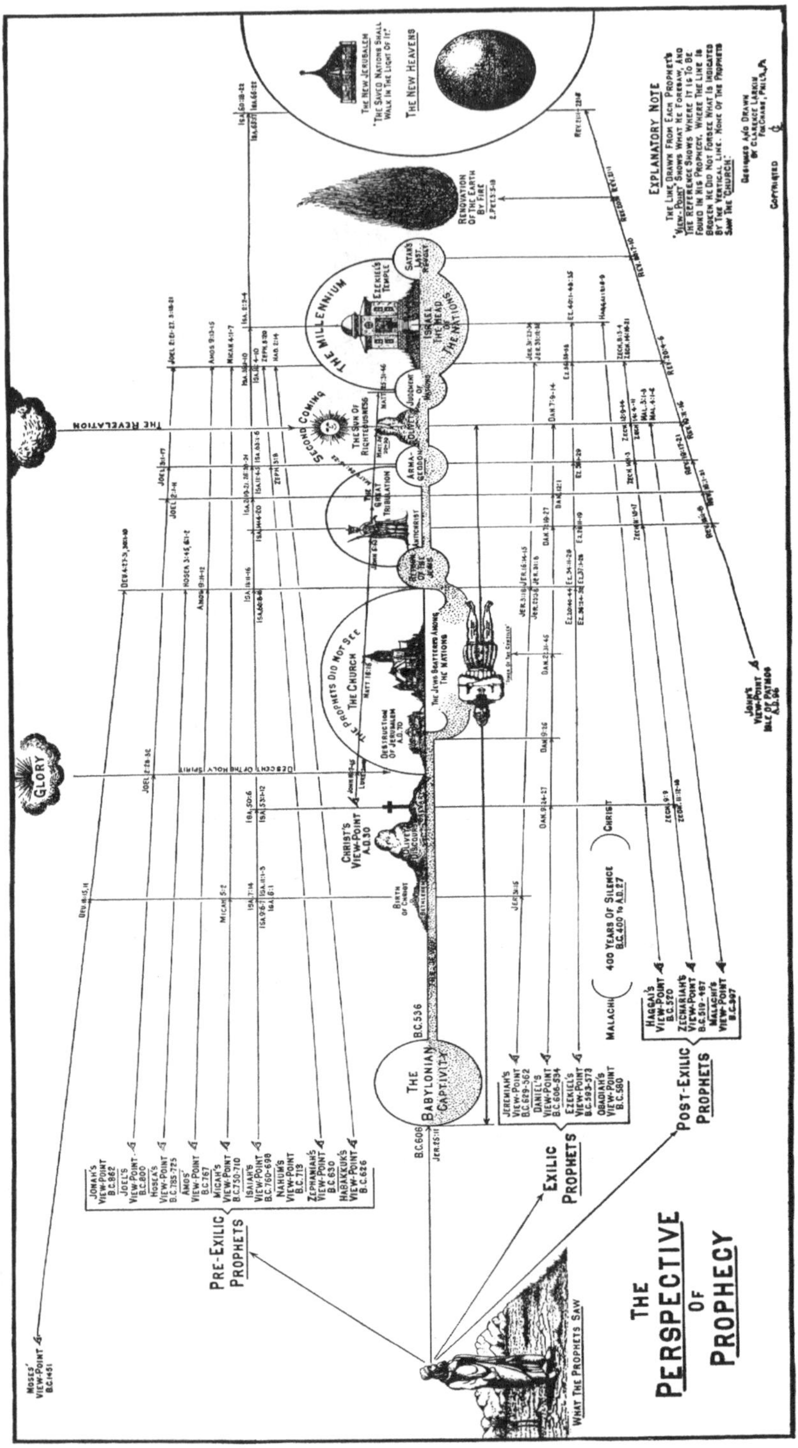
THE PERSPECTIVE OF PROPHECY
WHAT THE PROPHETS SAW
PRE-EXILIC PROPHETS
EXILIC PROPHETS
POST-EXILIC PROPHETS
THE BABYLONIAN CAPTIVITY
400 YEARS OF SILENCE
GLORY
THE REVELATION
SECOND COMING
THE MILLENNIUM
THE GREAT TRIBULATION
ARMA-GEDDON
EXPLANATORY NOTE

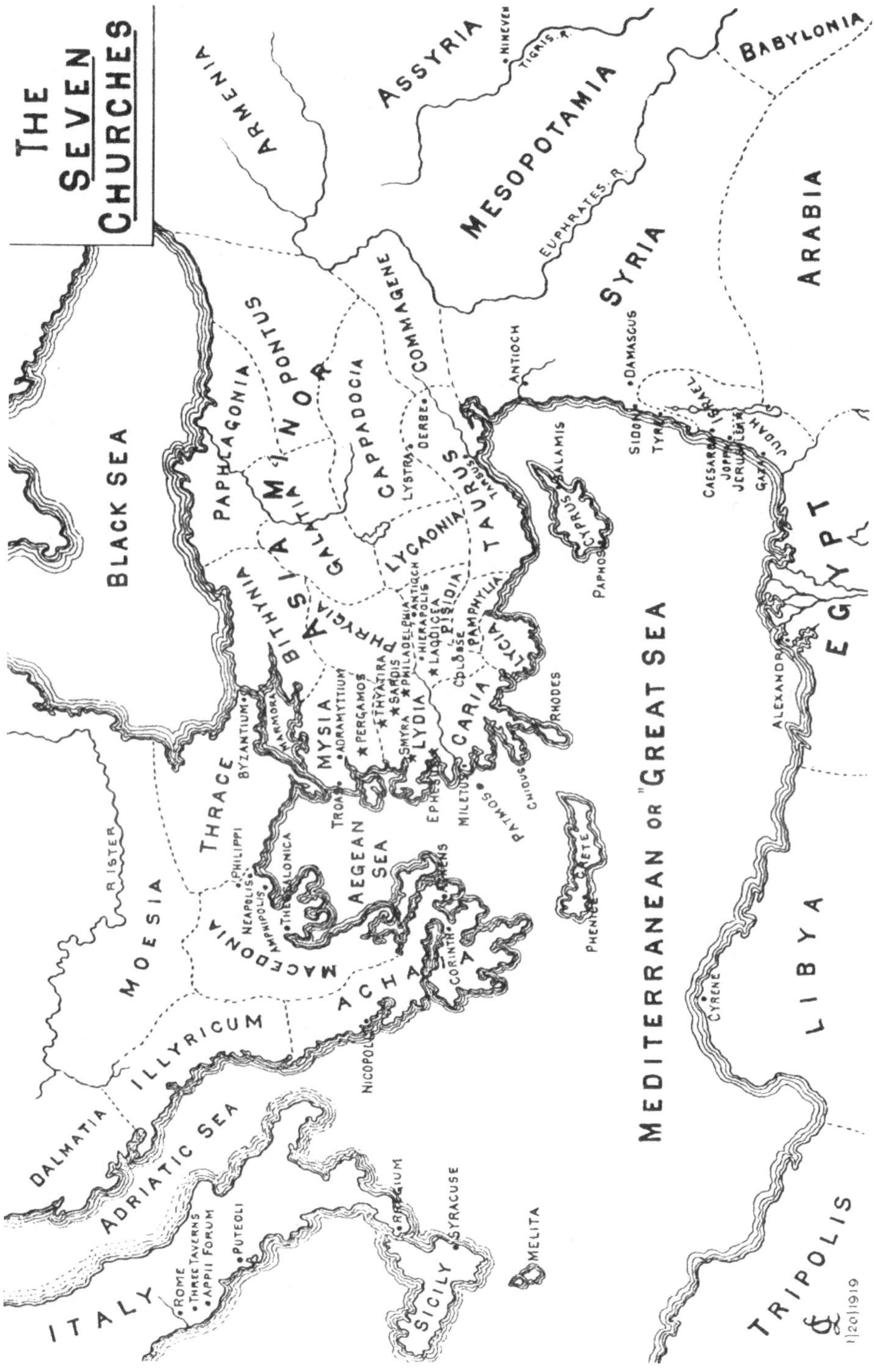
THE SEVEN CHURCHES
BLACK SEA
ARMENIA
ASSYRIA
NINEVEH
TIGRIS R.
BABYLONIA
MESOPOTAMIA
EUPHRATES R.
ARABIA
SYRIA
DAMASCUS
ANTIOCH
SIDON
TYRE
ISRAEL
JUDAH
CAESAREA
JOPPA
JERUSALEM
GAZA
EGYPT
ALEXANDRIA
PONTUS
PAPHLAGONIA
COMMAGENE
CAPPADOCIA
ASIA MINOR
GALATIA
BITHYNIA
LYCAONIA
TAURUS
TARSUS
LYSTRA
DERBE
PHRYGIA
PISIDIA
ANTIOCH
PAMPHYLIA
LYCIA
CARIA
LYDIA
MYSIA
HIERAPOLIS
LAODICEA
COLOSSE
PHILADELPHIA
SARDIS
THYATIRA
PERGAMOS
SMYRNA
EPHESUS
MILETUS
ADRAMYTTIUM
TROAS
MARMORA
BYZANTIUM
CYPRUS
SALAMIS
PAPHOS
RHODES
CNIDUS
PATMOS
CRETE
PHENICE
MEDITERRANEAN OR "GREAT SEA
AEGEAN SEA
THRACE
PHILIPPI
NEAPOLIS
AMPHIPOLIS
THESSALONICA
MACEDONIA
ATHENS
CORINTH
ACHAIA
MOESIA
R. ISTER
ILLYRICUM
NICOPOLIS
DALMATIA
ADRIATIC SEA
ITALY
ROME
THREE TAVERNS
APPII FORUM
PUTEOLI
RHEGIUM
SYRACUSE
SICILY
MELITA
LIBYA
CYRENE
TRIPOLIS
1|20|1919

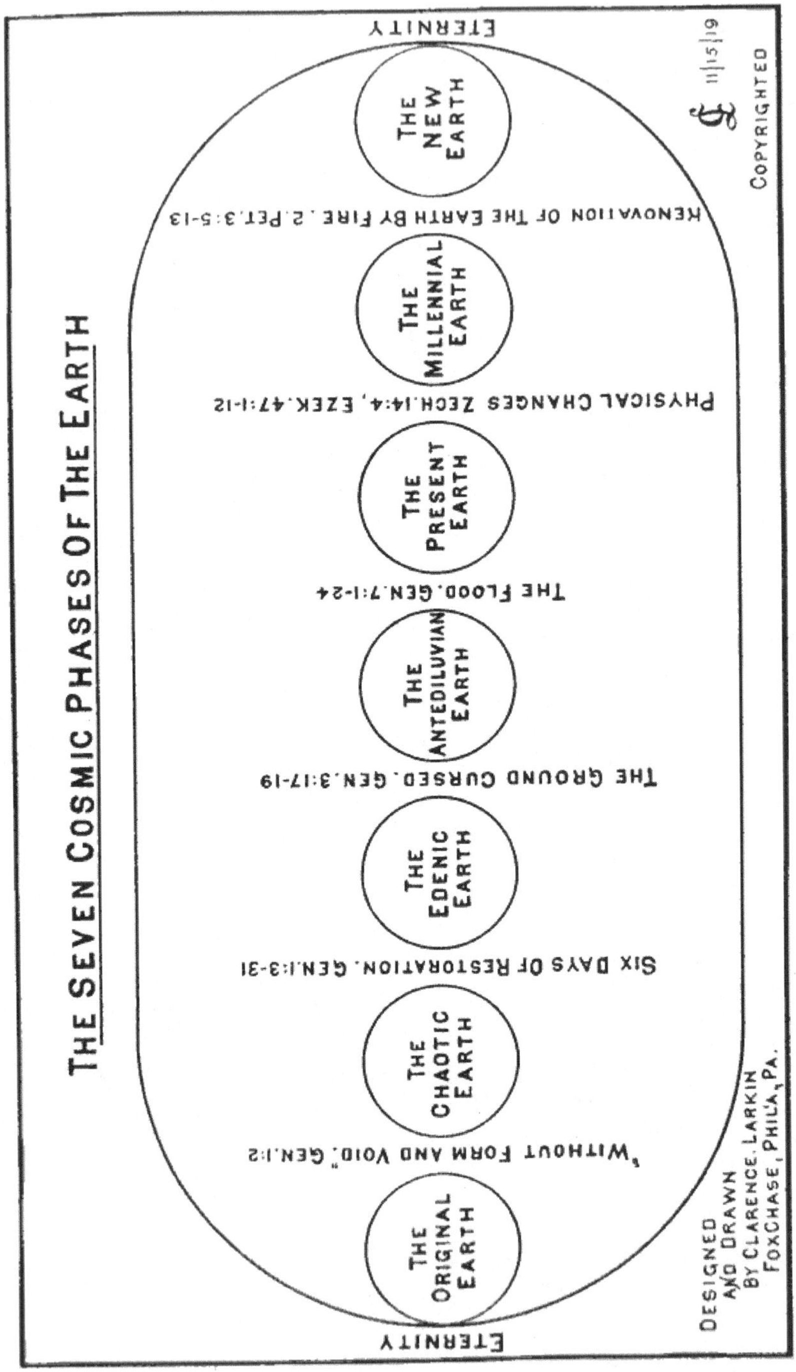

The Seven Cosmic Phases Of The Earth
Eternity
The Original Earth
"Without Form And Void." Gen.1:2
The Chaotic Earth
Six Days Of Restoration. Gen.1:3-31
The Edenic Earth
The Ground Cursed. Gen.3:17-19
The Antediluvian Earth
The Flood. Gen.7:1-24
The Present Earth
Physical Changes Zech.14:4, Ezek.47:1-12
The Millennial Earth
Renovation Of The Earth By Fire. 2.Pet.3:5-13
The New Earth
Eternity
Designed And Drawn By Clarence. Larkin Foxchase, Phila, Pa.
Copyrighted 11/15/19

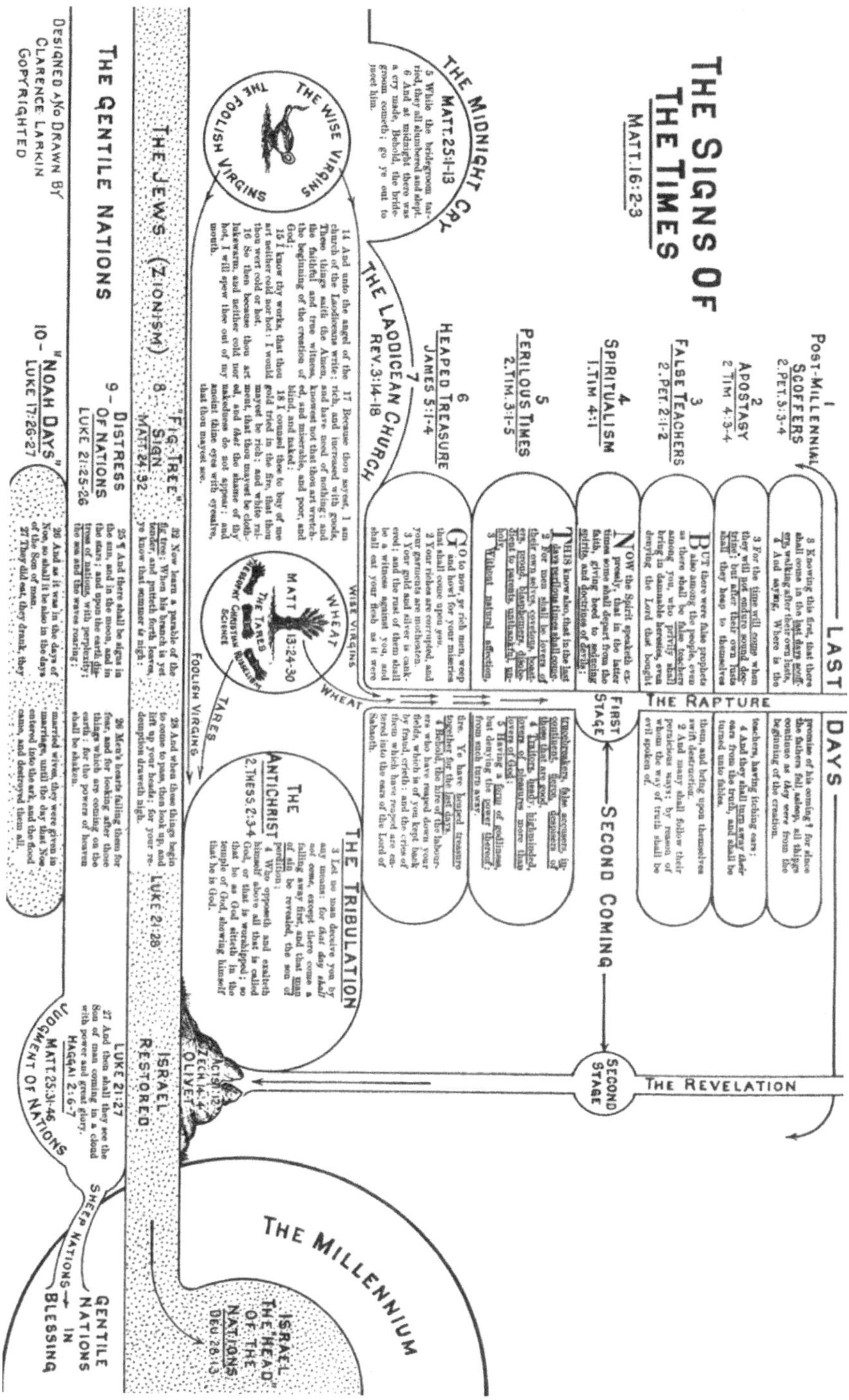
THE SIGNS OF THE TIMES
MATT.16:2-3
LAST DAYS
THE RAPTURE
FIRST STAGE
SECOND COMING
SECOND STAGE
THE REVELATION
1 POST-MILLENNIAL SCOFFERS 2.PET.3:3-4
2 APOSTASY 2 TIM 4:3-4
3 FALSE TEACHERS 2.PET.2:1-2
4 SPIRITUALISM 1.TIM 4:1
5 PERILOUS TIMES 2.TIM.3:1-5
6 HEAPED TREASURE JAMES 5:1-4
7 THE LAODICEAN CHURCH REV.3:14-18
THE MIDNIGHT CRY MATT.25:1-13
THE WISE VIRGINS
THE FOOLISH VIRGINS
WISE VIRGINS
FOOLISH VIRGINS
WHEAT
TARES
MATT 13:24-30
THE TRIBULATION
THE ANTICHRIST 2.THESS.2:3-4
THE JEWS (ZIONISM)
8 - "FIG TREE" SIGN MATT.24:32
LUKE 21:28
ISRAEL RESTORED
ACTS 1:12 ZECH.14:4 OLIVET
THE GENTILE NATIONS
9 - DISTRESS OF NATIONS LUKE 21:25-26
10 - "NOAH DAYS" LUKE 17:26-27
LUKE 21:27
HAGGAI 2:6-7
JUDGMENT OF NATIONS MATT.25:31-46
SHEEP NATIONS
GENTILE NATIONS IN BLESSING
THE MILLENNIUM
ISRAEL THE "HEAD" OF THE NATIONS DEU.28:13
DESIGNED AND DRAWN BY CLARENCE LARKIN COPYRIGHTED